Becoming

THE

PROFESSIONAL

WOMAN

25 Success Strategies to Prepare Women for the Business World

Edited by Linda Ellis Eastman

Goblin Fern Press
Madison, Wisconsin

Published by:
Goblin Fern Press, Inc.
3809 Mineral Point Road, Madison, WI 53705
Toll-free: 888-670-BOOK (2665)
www.goblinfernpress.com
Specializing in personalized publishing.
Quantity discounts available. Please contact the publisher.

ISBN-10: 1-59598-027-X
ISBN-13: 978-1-59598-027-4

Publisher's Cataloging-In-Publication Data
(Prepared by The Donohue Group, Inc.)

Becoming the professional woman : 25 success strategies to prepare women
for the business world / Linda Ellis Eastman, editor.

  p. : ill. ; cm. -- (Professional woman network series ; 1)
  ISBN-13: 978-1-59598-027-4
  ISBN-10: 1-59598-027-X

1. Businesswomen--United States--Life skills guides. 2. Women executives--
United States--Life skills guides. 3. Successful people--United States--Life
skills guides. 4. Success in business--United States--Handbooks, manuals,
etc. 5. Business etiquette--United States--Handbooks, manuals, etc. 6.
Career development--United States--Handbooks, manuals, etc. I. Eastman,
Linda Ellis.

HF5386 .B43 2005
620.1/082   2005930908

Cover and book design:
Bergerson Design   www.loisbdesigns.com
Aries Rising Productions   www.ariesrisingproductions.com

Printed in the United States of America
Second Printing

This book is dedicated to Angela Nash,
who lived her life with amazing grace.

TABLE OF CONTENTS

Introduction   ix
Linda Ellis Eastman

1. Personal Projection & Image   2
   DarLene Burkett

2. Believe in Yourself!   14
   Ruby Ashley

3. Getting the Job & Keeping It!   26
   Karlene Pedersen

4. Becoming Financially Savvy   34
   LaSonya McPherson Berry

5. Overcoming Obstacles   50
   Sharva Hampton-Campbell

6. Working in a Non-Traditional Work Environment   62
   Riki F. Lovejoy-Blaylock

7. Etiquette   72
   Linda Riser

TABLE OF CONTENTS
-CONTINUED-

8. Assertiveness Skills   84
Dr. Brenda Ward

9. Creating & Communicating Your Vision   96
Dr. Mamie Shields Norman

10. Starting Your Own Business   106
Elizabeth Waterbury

11. Networking & Visibility   120
Martha Barrett

12. Marketing Your Personal Brand   128
Nyda Bittmann-Neville

13. Wardrobe Organization   142
Laura Leezer

14. Male-Female Communication Styles   156
Myrtle Looby

15. Journaling for Personal & Professional Enrichment   170
Willie Joe Vary

16. Overcoming Negativity   186
Rosemary Bonilla

TABLE OF CONTENTS
-CONTINUED-

17. Communicate to Win   198
    Myralyn Stewart Miller

18. Transitioning into Management   212
    Mary Paul

19. Overcoming Fear   226
    Sharyn Yonkman

20. Understanding Diversity   242
    Diane Cain

21. From Challenge to Opportunity: 252
    Minority Women in the Workforce   *Dr. Karen Dace*

22. The Mind-Body Connection   260
    Dr. Carol Ann Ryser

23. The Power of You: Making a Positive Impact   276
    Dina Finta

24. Life Organization & Prioritizing   288
    Hazel Blake Parker

25. Leading the Way   300
    Dr. Danita Johnson-Hughes

ABOUT THE EDITOR

LINDA ELLIS EASTMAN

Linda Ellis Eastman is President & CEO of The Professional Woman Network (PWN), an International Training and Consulting Organization on Women's Issues. She has designed seminars which have been presented in China, the former Soviet Union, South Africa, the Phillipines, and attended by individuals in the United States from such firms as McDonalds, USA Today, Siemens-Westinghouse, the Pentagon, The Department of Defense, and the United States Department of Education.

An expert on Women's Issues, Ms. Eastman has certified and trained over one thousand women to start consulting/seminar businesses originating from such countries as Pakistan, the Ukraine, Antigua, Canada, Mexico, Zimbabwe, Nigeria, Bermuda, Jamaica, Costa Rica, England, South Africa, Malaysia, and Kenya. Founded in 1982 by Linda Ellis Eastman, The Professional Woman Network is committed to educating women on a global basis regarding self-esteem, confidence building, stress management, and emotional, mental, spiritual and physical wellness.

Ms. Eastman has been featured in *USA Today* and listed in *Who's Who of American Women,* as well as *Who's Who of International Leaders.* In addition to Women's Issues, Ms. Eastman speaks internationally regarding the importance of human respect as it relates to race, color, culture, age and gender. She will be facilitating an international conference in the fall of 2006 where speakers and participants from many nations will be able to discuss issues that are unique to women on a global basis.

Linda Ellis Eastman is also founder of The Professional Woman Speakers Bureau and The Professional Woman Coaching Institute. Ms. Eastman has dedicated her businesses to increasing the self-esteem and personal dignity of women and youth around the world.

Contact:
The Professional Woman Network
Post Office Box 333
Prospect, KY 40059
(502) 566-9900
lindaeastman@prodigy.net
www.prowoman.net
www.protrain.net

viii

INTRODUCTION

By Linda Ellis Eastman

The best way to learn about professionalism and how to enter the workplace is to ask women who have been there. As the President & CEO of The Professional Woman Network (PWN), I have come in contact with thousands of women who have wanted to know how they could network their way to the career of their dreams, develop a professional image, manage their finances, and increase self-esteem.

Women have a difficult time trusting other women. Often women who are in higher positions in the professional arena do not share their "trade" secrets with women entering the workforce. These women may not share because they wish to maintain control or power, and perceive the sharing of their knowledge as giving away power. This individual is often termed the "Queen Bee." The Queen Bee Syndrome is alive and very well in the business world. Because of this, younger women who are entering the professional arena may not have mentors to show them the way. It is because of this reason that this book has been written.

Therefore, I selected a number of PWN members who themselves were accomplished professionals with years of experience, and chose them to write a book which would be of value to you, the reader. A book which would give you various strategies for personal and professional success. A book which would help you on your journey to Becoming The Professional Woman.

The authors of this book feel very passionately about helping other women. The chapters have been authored by women including a physician, human resource director, educator, civil engineer, banker, training director, nurse, speech pathologist, social worker, construction company owner, and accountant. There are women in sales, an owner of a protocol school, and entrepreneurs who wish to share their trade secrets with you. These are the tips and strategies that will make your entry and journey within the professional workplace much smoother.

Many of the authors also own their own consulting practices and are highly experienced at helping women succeed both personally and professionally. I have personally known the writers of this book for many years and know that you will gain great personal and professional insight in the areas of attitude, appearance, behavior, entrepreneurship, and mental and emotional health. I wish you, the reader, the best of success as you take your steps to *Becoming The Professional Woman.*

Becoming

THE
PROFESSIONAL
WOMAN

ABOUT THE AUTHOR

DARLENE BURKETT

DarLene Burkett is a Corporate Trainer and Master Presenter having received national and international acclaim. She has worked as an Image Consultant and Makeup Artist for some of the world's leading cosmetic companies and fashion retailers.

With over twenty-five years of experience in the industry she has been featured in publications such as *Salon Sense, Sophisticate's Black Hair,* and *Heart & Soul.* Ms. Burkett has also been recognized by *Salon Sense* magazine for two consecutive years—2004 and 2005, being honored as one of the Black Women Power Brokers, "A Salute to Women Breaking Barriers in the Beauty Industry."

Ms. Burkett is the President and CEO of the Burkett Consulting Group (BCG), which specializes in diversity training, customer service, and professional imaging. BCG is dedicated to assisting individuals and corporations in pursuing professional excellence through one-on-one consultations, workshops, and seminars. Her mission is to restore customer service to the bygone level of excellence and prepare businesses to compete in a global workforce.

Ms. Burkett serves on the International Board of Advisors for the Professional Woman Network and is a member of the National Association of Female Executives.

Contact:
Burkett Consulting Group
20280 N. 59th Avenue
Suite 115-242
Glendale, Arizona 85308
(623) 825-9596
fax: (623) 825-9406
DarBurkett@aol.com

ONE

PERSONAL PROJECTION AND IMAGE

By DarLene Burkett

*"Your personal appearance and attitude is a snapshot
into your professional disposition."*

LIGHTS! – Expose your true self
• What do you want your image to say about you?

CAMERA! – Bringing the view of YOU into focus
• How do others perceive you?

ACTION! – Develop your best self
• Are you willing to do the work?

As children we daydreamed about what we wanted to be when we grew up. I can remember as a child being fascinated with movie stars and how they always looked so glamorous and well put together. They looked absolutely FLAWLESS and I daydreamed about becoming a star and having that same appeal. As I grew up I stepped out of *Fantasy Island* and moved into the *Real World,* realizing that a lot of hard work goes into accomplishing that image. You see, movies create an illusion and there is a lot of behind-the-scene preparation that goes into the making of a movie. The director may redo a scene numerous times before it becomes a wrap, before it becomes perfect, before it becomes flawless. However, in reality there are no double takes to making a first impression.

Your image is one of the most valued assets you possess. Your ability to effectively market yourself and leave a lasting impression within this global workforce could be the difference between a pat on the back or a promotion, a white-collar job or a pink slip, a corner office with a view or being stuck on the block. Corporations decide within moments if you are a good fit for their organization or not based upon their initial perception of you. By the time you leave the negotiation table you have been checked out and sized up from head to toe. Make no mistake about it, companies want the top talent. So, before you can make it to the boardroom you have to get past the casting couch.

My objective is to help you enhance or completely make over your personal projection and image through appearance, attitude and actions. My desire for you is that you will become informed and empowered to take the necessary steps in achieving an image that brings you enjoyment and personal satisfaction while enhancing your success in relationships both personally and professionally.

For starters, let's shine some LIGHT on what makes up your personal projection and image. Personal projection is the attribution of your ideas, feelings, character, and attitude. This includes your mannerisms and nonverbal emotional expressions. Your image is a representation or impression of your form, features, or personal style.

Your personal projection illuminates your image because the attitude you choose determines how others view you. Focused participation and dedication in your personal development will result in improving your professional disposition.

Your image is a reflection of you—it is the way other people see you, as if through a lens. It is what makes you unique; your nature, your composition. For example: a good image can determine whether people want to be around you or not, if you make friends easily, and how well you do in the business arena. A polished image builds great self-esteem and confidence. In short, your personal projection and image is your "D&A,"—your Disposition and Appearance.

GETTING INTO CHARACTER
Disposition
Your disposition is the culmination of your mind, body, and spirit that can and will fluctuate depending upon your internal and external circumstances. Your disposition effects your quality of life at work and home. So before you start your daily routine it is imperative that you choose your attitude which sets the tone for your day. For the most part we strive to always have a positive outlook on life. As nurturers we have the tendency of putting others' needs ahead of our own. Do you ever feel like things are so hectic that you have a problem balancing life's priorities? As we've all experienced some days are better than others; we're not feeling well, hormonal fluctuations, stress, and a number of other situations or occurrences can upset our balance. Between working, running a business, maintaining our home, taking care of our children and quality time with our significant other, it may be difficult to imagine a life that allows for all of the things that you would like to do. That's why it is important to schedule time for the main character—You.

Consider including one or both of these activities into your life to help keep balance and focus:

• Exercise is key to healthy living and helps to keep your mind, body, and spirit in sync, which in turn centers your disposition. Find an exercise that you enjoy, maybe walking, yoga, pilates, swimming, or hiking, just to name a few. The important thing is to do what works best for you to help you keep a positive disposition. If you feel good about your body, it reflects in your posture, the way you walk, and the way you interact with others.

• Keeping a journal can be like discovering a new best friend. You know how it feels when you have a good heart-to-heart talk with your best friend and it clears your head and you feel that all is right with the world. Jotting down your dreams and desires, fears and phobias, blunders and blessings can help to bring clarity to your vision and order to your life. For me over the years journaling has tracked the script of my life and what's most assuring is that my new best friend can be entrusted with my secrets. Clearing your head through journaling can be very therapeutic, which in return keeps you grounded, centered and focused.

Dress Rehearsal

Appearance

Your appearance is critical in projecting a positive image. Make a point to always look your best by creating a wardrobe that supports your lifestyle. Ensure your attire is appropriate for your age, size, and shape. Too often women try to hang on to their youth or a style that needs to be written out of the equation. Since in most business situations clothing covers over ninety percent of the body it is important to make a very powerful statement, presenting yourself at your best each and every time. This includes your attire, hair, nails, skin, and makeup.

What does your wardrobe say about you? If you stand in your closet frustrated trying to figure out what to wear, what fits, or you're purchasing a new outfit for every occasion, then it's time for a dress rehearsal. Invite a girlfriend over and have a wardrobe check, trying on your clothes and clearing out pieces that no longer fit or you have not worn in the past couple of years.

We tend to become attached to our things—a favorite sweater, the perfect pair of shoes, that power suit. I know for me, every item that I have purchased over time has been my favorite. It makes me feel fabulous each and every time I wear it. However, we must know when to let go. Donate items that you can no longer use to a woman's shelter or consider taking them to a consignment shop. Anything that you donate is tax deductible. Once you have cleared out the old you're now ready for the new.

You can look fabulous without spending a fortune if you shop wisely and follow some fundamental tried and true rules. In building your wardrobes here are some tips to help you select the best investment pieces for your budget:

- Make a list of your wardrobe needs and wants, concentrating on purchasing the needs first, unless of course you run across something on your wants list that is an incredible bargain. Just be careful, you don't want to buy something that will sit in your closet and you never wear it. Also, another word of caution, you want to make sure to only purchase items that compliment your body style.

- Think quality over quantity: Invest in high-quality pieces, made with great fabric and having classic lines, such as a suit made of wool, gabardine, or silk, instead of multiple items of lesser quality. Purchase the best quality you can afford; these items are timeless. You can always mix and match to expand an outfit and use accessories to complete the look and make your statement. Believe me, quality shows and wears well.

- Learn to shop "off season," January and July. You can get some great deals at the end of the season. Make a point of purchasing items that will not go out of style for a few seasons and keep fad items to a minimum.

If you are not sure what looks great on you or you'd like to change your style, get help from a professional image consultant. If you don't enjoy shopping, utilize the service of complimentary personal shoppers at the department stores and boutiques. An image consultant or personal shopper can save you a whole lot of time, money and frustration.

A key factor in completing our look is how well we maintain the foundation—our skin, hair and nails. These are areas that cannot be covered up with clothing and are exposed the majority of the time. Therefore, particular attention should be given to these areas. The comments I hear are, "I can't do all of this! Where do I find the time?" Well, I can tell you what I tell all my clients, "It's easier to keep up than to catch up! No one is perfect, but you can be flawless." Self-pampering is the one thing that women don't do enough of. Not only is being pampered relaxing, but it helps with establishing our mood and polishes our image.

Skin should look great with or without makeup. Some women feel that if they do not wear makeup it is not necessary to have a skin care regimen. Big mistake! Well-cared-for skin shows and will certainly be noticed, plus it becomes a great canvas should you decide to wear make-up. Caring for your skin and giving it the attention that it needs causes the makeup to look better and last longer.

Makeup should simply enhance your natural beauty. Think of cosmetics as being an extension of your wardrobe, a compliment to your style, something you wear every day. When applied properly it can work wonders. If you're not sure where to start or what to do, take some time and get a consultation or makeover from an expert at one of your local department stores. They are trained professionals and will help you with your individual needs. Here are some tips to help you keep up with the foundation of your image:

- A proper skin care regimen consists of daily cleansing, toning, moisturizing, facials, and acne control. Consider this preventive maintenance, something that will stay with you ensuring vibrant and problem-free skin.

- Choose a cleansing regimen that works for your skin type and addresses your specific skin care concerns. If you have oily and/or blemish-prone skin use products that are oil-free. Whereas, if you have dry skin, select products that are rich in emollients.

- Even though you are doing the daily maintenance of cleansing your skin, schedule monthly facials. A good aesthetician will educate you on your skin, address any anti-aging concerns and advise you on the latest treatments for specific skin conditions, such as adult acne, uneven tone, and overall skin rejuvenation.

- Exfoliation buffs away dead skin cells and leaves your skin looking refreshed with a radiant glow. Skin cells renew themselves every twenty-eight days. A gentle scrub with fine granules such as sugar works well on your face, whereas something a bit more coarse such as salt works well for your body. If you exfoliate your body prior to shaving your legs, you will get a much closer longer lasting shave.

- Your hairstyle should fit your lifestyle and should be one that you can maintain. People will definitely pay attention to an attractive precision cut and in most cases they will compliment you on it. When you go to a salon take along some pictures of hairstyles that you like. When you call for an appointment let the receptionist know that you would like extra time for a consultation. Your hair stylist will help you design a look that compliments you and will work with you on how to recreate the look in between cuts and salon visits, offering advice on which styling tools and products work best with your hairstyle. This could be one of your features that helps make your first impression a memorable one.

• It is said that you can tell the age of a woman from the look of her hands. With all of the wear and tear I put on my hands I wouldn't be surprised if people could read the mileage. In my profession I'm washing my hands or using disinfectant wipes constantly, which causes them to be rough, dry, and cracked. A lot of value is weighted on your handshake so it's no wonder I used to get paranoid whenever I shook someone's hand. Now after I cleanse my hands I have a habit of immediately coating them with a rich emollient cream to soften and provide a protective moisture barrier. Keep hand creams and lotions in "drop zones": handbag, car, briefcase, desk, nightstand, so that you don't get caught with "man hands."

• Well-manicured nails speak for themselves with or without polish and are the perfect accoutrements to soft supple hands. Your nails should always be clean and neatly filed. Polish should not be chipped, even if it's clear polish—believe me, it's noticeable. Biting your nails or picking at the cuticles are bad habits and can wreck your image. If you don't have the time to do your nails at home, treat yourself to a manicure at a salon.

I remember one time as I was preparing to leave for a business trip I was running around trying to be superwoman making sure that I did everything around the house: check and reply to all of my emails, pick up my dry cleaning, the list went on and on. Inevitably I ran out of time and couldn't get my nails done before I left, so for me, this was not a good thing. I had to go from the airport directly to a meeting with a new client, and even though I was prepared for the meeting and looked flawless, my disposition was off. I was so self-conscious about my nails drawing attention during my presentation that whenever possible I sat there with my hands folded and hidden under the table. As soon as that meeting was over, I made a mad dash to the closest nail salon. Lesson learned!

- Paying attention to the small details makes a huge difference, because what you miss others will surely notice. For example, if you notice a run in your hosiery as you're getting dressed, don't just turn the run around so that it faces the inside of your leg, as that doesn't make it invisible. I guarantee you that someone will notice it and you will be self-conscious of it all day.

- When it comes to that fabulous image of yours, the bottom line is that you're interested in looking good and feeling great about yourself. Do what it takes to make it happen. Have fun with it! Get moving with an exercise routine that you enjoy, find a friend to walk with, you'll be amazed at how much stress you can release from exercising and how much energy you will gain.

- Break down and get started on cleaning out your closet. The sooner you get organized the sooner you can go shopping. Gain that competitive advantage by wearing the colors and styles that flatter your own coloring and body shape and notice your confidence growing at the same time.

Preventive maintenance can save you a whole lot of time and money. Make sure to take care of yourself. Keep your hair clean and neat at all times, maintain well-groomed hands and nails. This is work, but well worth it. Of all the decisions you make, none are more important to your accomplishments and satisfaction than the decisions you make about yourself. The things you conceive about yourself dictate how successful you are in every area of your life—personally, professionally, socially and spiritually.

Now that you've been informed and equipped with some useful suggestions and practical ways to make it easier for you to refine your personal projection and image, as well as becoming more aware of your professional style, it's time to take action. If you check yourself out in the mirror once, then it won't hurt to do it twice. Trust me, others will.

Your personal appearance and attitude is a snapshot into your professional disposition. Success comes in a series of snapshots that get played out on the movie screen of life of which you are the star.

Lights! Camera! Action!

You're on.

Notes:

_____

_____

_____

_____

_____

_____

_____

_____

_____

_____

_____

_____

_____

_____

_____

_____

_____

_____

_____

_____

_____

ABOUT THE AUTHOR

RUBY ASHLEY, M.B.A.

Ms. Ruby Ashley, is the Chief Executive Officer of Ruby Ashley & Associates. She is a leader in personal and professional development, specializing in the delivery of workshops, seminars, training programs and assessments. Her workshops and training programs are highly interactive and stimulating with focus on improving employee performance. She firmly believes that as long as individuals are willing to learn, change, and grow, they will always reach high levels of achievement.

Ms. Ashley is an accomplished motivational keynote speaker, facilitator, trainer, and consultant with more than 26 years of experience in the corporate environment. As a Certified Customer Service Trainer, she delivers an outstanding Customer Service Excellence program. Some of the other areas of training programs include Personal and Professional Development, Women's Issues, Diversity and Multiculturalism, Self-Esteem, Leadership Development, Strategic Planning, Road Map to Retirement, and Team Building. Teen topics are Save Our Youth, Teen Image, and Leadership.

Ms. Ashley earned a Bachelor of Science and Masters Degree in Business from Brenau University in Gainesville, GA. She is a member of The Professional Woman Network, a certified trainer, and a member of The PWN International Advisory Board. The Professional Woman Network has more than 22 years of experience in the professional development field conducting seminars and workshops for Fortune 500 companies, universities, professional organizations, and governmental agencies. She holds memberships in other various professional organizations, including the American Business Woman Association, Toastmasters International, Les Brown Speaker's Bureau, and an Affiliate of Leadership Development Group, Inc. She is a youth mentor and an active volunteer in her community.

Contact:
Ruby Ashley
Ruby Ashley & Associates
P.O. Box 312383
Atlanta, GA 31131
(404) 349-0458
rbyash@aol.com
www.protrain.net

TWO

BELIEVE IN YOURSELF AND ACHIEVE!

By Ruby Ashley

Do you believe that you will reach your ultimate potential in life? Are you achieving all that you desire? If you think you are not reaching your capacity for achieving, you're right. Ninety-five percent of all people will achieve only five percent of their full potential. Why will they achieve so little, when their potential is so great?

The toughest questions are not necessarily those asked by other people, but the questions we ask ourselves. These are questions such as: What do I really want out of life? Do I have what it takes to get what I want? Why am I afraid to believe in myself? We often find ourselves afraid to pursue our passion in life because we don't believe we have what it takes to "Achieve in life what we want." Believing in yourself is the beginning of a change that will help you achieve whatever it is you want out of life.

Believing is Powerful!

Believing is acquired, not inborn. Finding the courage and confidence to believe in yourself is often a challenge. It is a challenge engulfed with negative messages and hurt from experiences that caused low self-esteem while robbing us of the feelings of self-worth needed to create happy, successful, and fulfilling lives as adults. Self-esteem has many definitions. I believe it has to do with personal beliefs that we have developed about ourselves. These beliefs include how our body looks, our work, our pay, and how we rate ourselves as being attractive. Too often, we have negative beliefs that follow us from childhood into adulthood. These negative beliefs are the root cause of many of our failures in life. For some people, because they were overweight and self-conscious as a child, they carry this acceptance of a negative self-image into adulthood. We must from time to time re-examine our current personal belief system and get rid of the negative messages that produce feelings of self-doubt, replacing them with powerful positive messages. When your self-esteem is low, you must be willing to make the necessary changes to improve how you feel.

Believing in yourself requires knowing that your life has value, and as long as you are in this world, you are valuable and all things are possible for your life.

How can you begin to increase belief in yourself?

1. **Get positive encouragement from others.** It is important to surround yourself with people who make you feel good about yourself, share your vision and inspire you.

2. **Give yourself internal encouragement.** Concentrate on saying positive things to yourself, do volunteer work, mentor, work out, take

a class, listen to motivational tapes, read inspirational books and the Bible. Do worthy things that make you feel good about yourself.

3. **Take a break.** We often blame ourselves for hard times. There will be times when you will go through down cycles in your life. Know that you are not alone, everyone experiences down periods. You should not assume responsibility for matters that are out of your control.

4. **Your appearance says a lot about how you see yourself.** Having a down and out day? Dress as though you feel like a million dollars. I know this works. I have tried it many times. You will be surprised at how looking good can help you feel good!

5. **Accept responsibility.** You must make a commitment to not only believe, but to do what is required of you to keep the wheels of progress moving smoothly.

6. **Affirm yourself.** Affirmations work. Repeat the following affirmation out loud to yourself three times each morning and three times at night, "I have power and will use it to create the outcome I desire. I will use my power wisely for I expect the best!" Repeating your affirmation can implant the words within your sub-conscious that will be there to help you combat any negative self-talk and self-doubt, and help you achieve your goal.

When you believe something, you've got power! Have you ever wondered why some people seem to have more control over their lives than others? It's not that they never have challenges, but somehow through positive expectancy they are able to overcome those challenges and lead victorious successful lives.

Many things will happen to you in your life that will require you to believe and have faith that you can overcome whatever stands in your way. My mother became critically ill when I was a small child. Just before my mother died, she asked my grandmother to raise my sister and me. My grandmother had a great heart, but little money. I had a difficult childhood and had to help contribute money to the family to survive. At the age of ten, I was introduced to working in the cotton, pea, and tomato fields. The days were long, hard and hot. The sun was so hot, I had to wear a scarf on my head to stay cool in the blistering heat. I remember standing in the cotton field, looking at the sun thinking and believing that one day I would get out of those fields and go to college and get a good job. I was determined not to stay in those fields. I pictured myself with a college education, with nice clothes, a nice home, and providing for my grandmother. I learned to look past my current condition and picture a bright future away from working in those fields. I'll never forget the moment when I made that commitment to myself to change my life. I had to look beyond my circumstances and believe in my heart that I could truly achieve my dreams. You can do the same! One of my favorite quotes is:

"You are a valuable, significant person although your circumstances may have you feeling otherwise."

—James W. Newman

Positive Self-Image

When you look in the mirror, what do you see? A person who can accomplish anything, or someone who has great ambitions, but many limitations? Self-image is an important part of your "Belief System." If you've been programmed all of your life to be average, and you believe that you are, then what you believe will become your reality. The first step to achieving whatever you want in life begins with the ability to see yourself stripped of limitations. Living up to self-imposed limiting expectations will keep you going in circles all of your life. You must see yourself accomplishing your goals.

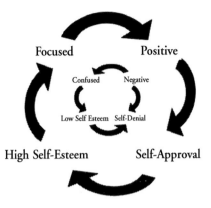

"Things do not change; we change."
—Henry David Thoreau

Positive Thinking

Most of us believe that we are positive thinkers, yet eighty percent of our "self-talk" is negative. We talk to ourselves at a rate of 600 to 800 words per minute. You have to be aware of what you are saying or thinking to yourself. Are you negative or positive?

Remember, we move toward whatever thoughts dominate our mind. Whenever you have a negative thought, you will need to change it into a positive thought in order to succeed.

The following statement is an example of changing a negative thought into a positive thought. "I'll never achieve my goal," into "I can and will achieve my goal!" Self-talk is significant in achieving whatever you want! Words and thoughts are powerful tools that control our lives. For instance, your emotional state is determined by the kinds of thoughts you are thinking. If you feel down and out, nearly every reaction you have to things around you will be colored negatively.

When you have been knocked down in life, you tend to see only the worst in people, in situations and in your options. When you are feeling hopeless, it will really take hold if you don't change the way you feel. Monitor your emotions and recognize when you are in this state of mind. Some people call it "having the blues." When I am in this state, I go out of my way to purposely compliment others to make them feel good.

I recommend you recall an event that was hilarious or something funny that will be uplifting to your spirit. When I need a good laugh, I always think about the "Six Flags Over Georgia" amusement park, where my friends and I have had many memorable experiences. One such experience I always think about is the parachute ride that I was "enjoying" with a friend who was still screaming after the ride had come down and stopped. She had her eyes closed and mouth open screaming. I was laughing so hard, I couldn't get her to stop. Finally, the ride operator touched her and said, "The ride has stopped. You're back on the ground." That was the highlight of our trip, and to this day we both still laugh about the parachute ride. (It was a relief to know I was not the only one who did a lot of screaming on rides.)

We cannot always control the thoughts that come into our minds, but we can control the thoughts that we dwell on. As Shakespeare said, "There is nothing either good or bad, but thinking makes it so." Learning to recognize emotionally distorted thinking is key to controlling your state of mind. When you build a strong belief system that is powerful and positive in your mind, it will allow you to propel past the negative situations.

How you begin and end your day is important. Start each day with positive thoughts and focus on your goals. End your day the same way. Whatever you focus on intently will eventually become your reality.

That's because your thoughts direct your actions and your actions define your life. Hint: Dream about how you are going to accomplish your goal.

While you are dreaming, visualize in detail using all of your senses, taste, touch, sound, smell, as well as sight. Now, imagine how you will feel after accomplishing your goal: the triumph, satisfaction, or excitement you associate with starting your own business, writing a book, speaking in front of millions of people, hosting your own talk show, investing in your health, or purchasing your dream home. Just before you get up in the morning, visualize what you are going to do that day to help achieve your goal. In other words, like a puzzle, accomplish your goal a piece at a time.

Self-Discipline

It will be virtually impossible to achieve your goals without determination, self-discipline, and desire. When I was a teenager I was faced with failing to reach the goal that I set as a child. That goal was to finish high school and go to college. I also wanted to obtain an undergraduate and a graduate degree before the age of 40. I succeeded in getting my undergraduate degree at the age of 39, but had to make a serious decision when I set the goal to get the graduate degree by age 40. That goal not only required self-discipline but determination. The graduate program was a two-year program. Reality was, I had to give up many privileges in order to make that goal a reality. At the beginning of the school year, my professor called me into his office and voiced his concern. The fact I was a part-time student taking a full load was not permissible. I talked my professor into letting me take the courses with the agreement that if I failed to meet the grade requirement, I would reduce my number of classes. I began the program in the fall and received my graduate degree in May...eight days before my 40th birthday. The achievement of this goal not only came with self-discipline, but began with a strong Belief System that I could and I would prevail in obtaining my degree. When you have a goal, challenge yourself and you will be amazed at what you can accomplish.

Reaching your full potential means that you'll have to see your life's work as a race without a finish line. High achievers do not view the pursuit of their potential as a nine-to-five job. They instead, see it as their life's work, striving to beat their own personal best...time and time again.

Be Relentless

Don't give up. If you've got a goal, product or idea that you really want to be successful, you've got to be relentless. Most people don't realize that if you have something you want to do, if it's your passion, and you want to excel, you may have to talk to a lot of people before you can find someone who will buy into your passion. As Spanish philosopher Jose Ortega y Gassett pointed out, "Our lives have at all times been before all else the consciousness of what we can do." Where are you going? What is the future bringing you? More importantly, what are you bringing to the future? It is not so much where you are, but where are you moving right now? Is your life moving up? Or is it moving down? In whatever direction it's going, you are in control. If you want to begin to turn things around, because it's not what you want it to be, then it's going to require perseverance on your part. Longfellow said that "Perseverance is a great element of success." To you the reader, I dedicate the "I BELIEVE" poem to you.

I BELIEVE

I Believe there are talents and gifts inside of me.
I Believe I can transform my obstacles and challenges into victory.
I Believe if my goals are going to be, it's up to me.
I Believe in this world, I am destined to make a difference.
I know I am going to achieve, because I believe and now
I must proceed.

—Ruby Ashley

The series of questions which follow will help you achieve your goals. What would you like to accomplish now, which would give you a great feeling of achievement?

_____

_____

_____

What do you believe has kept you from achieving your goal so far? (Why haven't you achieved it already?)

_____

_____

_____

What strengths will you be able to call upon to help you achieve your goal?

_____

_____

_____

Who can you call upon now to support you in achieving your efforts?

_____
_____
_____

What strategy will you use, or what will you tell yourself when you have a setback or disappointment?

_____
_____
_____

What will it take from you to reach that point of achievement?

_____
_____
_____

When will you take the first step to achieve it?

_____
_____
_____

How will you track it?

_____
_____
_____

Congratulations on believing and achieving your goal!

Goal Completed_____

Notes:

_____

_____

_____

_____

_____

_____

_____

_____

_____

_____

_____

_____

_____

_____

_____

_____

_____

_____

_____

_____

_____

ABOUT THE AUTHOR

KARLENE PEDERSEN

I would like to dedicate this chapter to my two grand-daughters, Kayla and Deanna Bailey, who will be entering their careers in the near future, and to my two daughters, Lisa Giraudi who is an accomplished business woman and Rachelle Bailey who is just entering the business world. A special thanks to the High School Seniors who met with me to discuss some of the things they would like to know as they journey towards their careers, and to the young business ladies who responded to my question "what do you wish you had known before entering the business world."

Karlene (Ewing) Pedersen serves on the International Advisory Board for The Professional Woman Network and is a member of The Professional Woman Speakers Bureau. Ms. Pedersen's career in Human Resources includes having served as Director of Human Resources for several healthcare facilities, Corporate Human Resources Director, Surgery Center Director. She has been involved in several start-up programs and hospital mergers. In 1990 she started her own consulting business, KE Consulting, which has been primarily focused on healthcare facilities. In this chapter, she speaks with much authority, having interviewed several thousand applicants over the past twenty years, and developing extensive experience in employee investigations.

Karlene Pedersen

Contact:
KE Consulting
P.O. Box 22395
Bakersfield, CA 92290
(559) 731-1051
kewing100@aol.com
www.protrain.net

THREE

GETTING THE JOB AND KEEPING IT

By Karlene Pedersen

Choosing a career path will be one of the major factors affecting your life. Successful accomplishment can be made easier by beginning to prepare yourself NOW. This chapter will guide you through the process of choosing a career, preparing yourself, interviewing, and ultimately getting the job and keeping it.

Preparing for your future
• What do you enjoy doing that would have value in the business world?
• What is your passion?
• Can you make a living by following your own interests or hobbies?
• Believe in yourself and abilities (talents).
• Don't put yourself down.
• Build your confidence by volunteering in community and church activities.
• Develop an honest value system and conscience. Our conscience gives us integrity. Listen to that still small voice inside you.

Prepare Yourself

• Personality Tests. Personality tests help you define a career that fits you, and also provides a guide for the type of personalities you can work with the best.

• Understand your personal value.

• Develop good "word habits." Using such words as "I just…" or "I'm sorry, but…" preceding a statement diminishes the value or force of what you say and expresses a negative attitude.

• Volunteer. Be active in your church and community. Volunteer activities will prove to be as valuable on your future resume as "paid" work, and can also be a guide to help you decide on the type of work you enjoy and get the most satisfaction from.

Designing an eye-catching resume

Prepare a concise, easy-to-read resume that clearly defines your education, past experiences (both volunteer and employment), community involvement, and future goals. Make sure there are no misspelled words and use proper grammar and sentence structure. References can be listed on a separate sheet of paper, or simply state at the end of your resume that "References will be supplied upon request." Put your name, address, and telephone number centered at the top of the first page, as well as any other contact information, such as fax, cell phone, or e-mail address.

If you are mailing the resume, it must be accompanied with a short (typed) letter which clearly defines the position that you are interested in being considered for. Sign the letter just above your typed name at the end of the letter. Place the resume and letter, unfolded, in a large envelope. If you are responding to an advertisement, be sure to state this in the cover letter. Example: I am submitting my resume to be considered for _____ position which was in the (name of paper, magazine) on (date). Be sure to follow directions (if any) for submitting your resume.

If you do not hear from the company, then feel free to follow up with a short letter or telephone call stating when you sent your resume and emphasize your interest in working for their company.

One resume does not fit all

• A common mistake many people make is to use the same resume for every position they apply for.

• The resume will be the first step in the job selection process and if it does not spark an interest in the reader, the process will end there.

• Design the resume to fit the position and the company.

Preparing for the Interview

• Have a clear understanding of the position and the company. Good resources are the library, internet, Chamber of Commerce and Better Business Bureau. If they have a product—use it so you can talk about it. If they publish a magazine—read it thoroughly.

• Have questions clearly in your mind that you can ask about the company, or comments that you can make about the position and/or company. Rehearse in front of the mirror or with a friend so that you will be comfortable. Elicit feedback from a friend as to how you express yourself, and work on any deficiencies so you will be able to express yourself clearly during the interview.

• A common mistake is not being prepared to answer the question "what are your weaknesses?"

• Check out the location of the interview, the traffic, the parking and allow extra time to get to the interview. Heavy traffic is not a legitimate excuse for being late.

- The three languages of an interview are body, verbal and appearance. All are equally important.

Body Language

- Sit back in your chair.

- Do not slouch.

- Keep your hands comfortably in your lap.

- Avoid twiddling your thumbs or quick, sudden movements.

- Sit with legs crossed at the ankles or together with feet on floor.

- Look attentively at the interviewer, but don't stare and do not continually look down as if embarrassed.

Verbal Language

During the interview, the interviewer will be evaluating how you communicate verbally.

- Practice using good English which not only means the words you select but also the grammar. "I don't have any" instead of "I don't got any."
- Speak positively rather than negatively or in an apologetic manner.
- Know the language of the position and the company.

Appearance

You want to be neat and professionally groomed but not overdressed for the position or the company. A tailored look is always appropriate. Slinky or revealing clothing is never appropriate for an interview.

- Check your appearance in a full-length mirror. Is your clothing neat and clean? Are the colors coordinated? Are your shoes polished and clean?

• Are your fingernails clean and well-manicured?

• Is your hair clean and well-groomed with an appropriate style for the position you are interviewing for?

• Your makeup should be conservative in color and application.

The Interview

Arrive a few minutes early (never late). Announce your name clearly to the receptionist and state the name of the person you have an appointment with. Be very courteous and friendly, but do not engage in "giggly" chit-chat which indicates your nervousness.

• Make sure you know the correct pronunciation and spelling of the name of the interviewer.

• Never take another person to the interview with you.

• Look the interviewer in the eye and greet him/her with a firm hand shake and a warm smile.

• Do not sit until you have been directed to do so.

• Take a deep breath and relax.

• Be personable, listen carefully, and show interest.

• Do not interrupt the interviewer.

• Be honest. It is better to say "I do not know" than to make up an answer or respond with incorrect information about your experience.

• Don't trash the company's competitors or other applicants. This shows insecurity on your part and that you probably will not be a good team player.

• Don't put yourself down. If you have received praise for work you have done, admit it, but don't boast about it.

Concluding the Interview

The interviewer is the one who concludes the interview—not the interviewee.

- You will usually be asked if you have any other questions or comments regarding the job.

- If there are none that you can think of, don't just say "no." Rather express your appreciation for the time spent with you in explaining the policies and position applied for.

- Tell the interviewer that you are interested in the job and that you look forward to hearing from the company.

- After the interview send a hand-written note to the interviewer expressing your appreciation for the interview and stating your interest in the position.

- If you do not hear from the company in ten days, it would be appropriate to follow up with a telephone call.

Keeping the Job

Companies are looking for employees who are capable, willing, and enthusiastic about being a part of a team to advance the future goals of the company.

- Be flexible and willing to learn and follow the routines in the job.

- Be a team player—not a loner only interested in advancing your own agenda.

- Show your dependability by being punctual and doing your best in all that you are asked to do.

- Do not get caught up in gossip and jealousy which is destructive to everyone and cannot help you perform to your best level.

• Always be honest and straightforward.

• If you make a mistake, admit it.

• If you don't understand something, ask for help or clarification.

Making yourself valuable to the company

• Volunteer for special assignments.

• Learn as many functions of the company as you can.

• Join professional and community organizations and participate actively in them.

• Take classes and advance your knowledge and skills.

Work each day, each project as though it is a stepping stone to your future. Think before reacting, and don't burn your bridges. You never know who is watching you. Don't hold a grudge. Always remember in the workplace, you are a "business *person*" not a "business *woman*" and you will normally be treated accordingly.

If you will follow the steps outlined in this chapter and believe in yourself, there is no limit to the success you can achieve.

ABOUT THE AUTHOR

LaSonya McPherson Berry

LaSonya Berry is an entrepreneur, trainer, consultant and personal/professional mentor. She is a dynamic speaker and motivator who inspires individuals to reach their potential. LaSonya has a BS in Industrial Engineering, Masters in Human Resource Development, and will complete her doctorate in 2008. She has obtained certification in Leadership, Personal Development, Diversity and is a certified Youth Trainer.

Prior to starting McPherson, Berry & Associates, Inc., LaSonya began her career as a counselor. She became a charter member of Jasper County Teen Peer Counselors. She was trained to counsel in areas of teen pregnancy, drug abuse, peer pressure and all adolescent situations. LaSonya worked with the Department of Social Services with their teen pregnancy program, and facilitated workshops with teenagers who were a product of generational mothers of teen pregnancy. After obtaining her degrees, she worked in Human Resources for GE and held various leadership positions with IBM for over 10 years.

LaSonya understands the need for community involvement. She is an alumna of the United Ways' Volunteer Involvement Program that provides board training. Her community involvement and training resulted in a director position for Operation Dignity's Bankhead Courts Human Resource Center. The center offered training classes that were parallel to the Welfare to Work Program and that is what inspired LaSonya to start GET POISED, a training and development business designed to help people reach their destiny. She obtained additional training, certification and became affiliated with The Professional Woman Network, an international training organization, as an International Advisory Board member and trainer. The business was later expanded and became McPherson, Berry & Associates, Inc. She currently serves as president.

Contact:
McPherson, Berry & Associates, Inc.
P.O. Box 360669, Decatur, GA 30036
(404) 243-7926
fax: (404) 241-5795
www.mcphersonberryassoc.com
lasonya@mcphersonberryassoc.com
www.protrain.net

FOUR

BECOMING FINANCIALLY SAVVY

By LaSonya McPherson Berry

Your financial health should be as important as your physical health. Being financially savvy rests on one important factor: what choices are you making? Do you want to enjoy now or forever? Do you want long-term benefits or short-term happiness? Only you can determine how successful you will be with your financial goals. This chapter provides some foundational strategies to help you reach your goals and financial potential. "Money is the root of all evil." This verse has been interpreted in many different ways. Money is not bad but how you *choose* to use it can be less favorable. The mentioning of the word "money" brings a smile to many and immediate tension to others. Most have it but not all of us are satisfied with the amount we have or what we can get with what we have.

Spending money is a pacifier to happiness. Do not get me wrong. I understand buying yourself something to celebrate success or because it is on sale. Two things are important in this celebration: can you afford it or will it bring you sadness later? Secondly, is the accomplishment worth celebrating? Is it a grand thing or will it take you off your financial goal path? Research has linked spending to emotions. It pays to think a second before you spend. It is important to keep your personal goals in mind as you make choices daily.

If at no other time in our life, we should understand that money and credit worthiness can be trying. We should think of them like relationships. They will need continuous care and nurturing. Things will go wrong. Put a plan of action in place to correct the situation or put you back on the right path. It is no secret that we as women splurge. We need to know when to splurge and have a limit to our splurging. Instead of buying some new clothing, what can you find in your closet that you haven't worn in a while? You can put a new twist to your ensemble by adding a brooch or a scarf. Another way would be to curtail your spending, perhaps by simply treating yourself to lunch. That is one way to celebrate and wean yourself off lavish spending.

This chapter will provide you with information and tips to assist you with your financial goals. We are never too young or too old to put an action plan into place. The information provided in this chapter will provide tips and ideas for you to personally implement into your wealth-building strategies. Let us begin with a tool I like to use to gauge where you are and where you are going. This tool is a budget.

A Budget a.k.a. Household Report

I have developed a budget spreadsheet tool I like to call "The Household Report." It is the same report companies use to take a snapshot view of their operations expenses. I believe we need to run our household finances just as a business would. It is a valuable report that is monitored monthly. You should begin by first setting up your home office. The home office's most crucial aspect is the filing system. It will help you organize warranties, assist with tax preparation and aid in the purchase of a home.

Begin by preparing a file folder for every bill that you pay. Once you set up the folders, group them by household expenses and variable expenses. Household expenses are mortgage, rent, utilities, auto loan and insurance premiums. They are the things that *must* be paid for the household to function. Other expenses such as credit cards, salon expenses and other loans would fall into another category. Lastly, you should have a folder for tax preparation material. This would be for any receipts or documents that could assist you during tax preparation time. Developing this filing system will assist you in the event of a tax audit or as you prepare to purchase a home. Having things simplified contributes to the plan we are trying to achieve of being savvy.

Now that you have everything organized, you are ready to set up your report. Take a look at the example provided.

Adjust the spreadsheet to include all of your expenses. Be sure to include the actual amount of each payment for fixed expenses. For those that are not fixed, include an estimated amount. The "Actual" column would be used to input the actual amount paid. It will be helpful to include the due date of each item. The "Status" column would be used to indicate where you are that month with payment. A check mark would indicate that it has been paid. Leave it blank if it has not been paid. The last column is for notes. Here I like to include account numbers, payment information (online or by phone) and account contact numbers.

The Household Report can be inserted into your planner for quick retrieval. Because it contains confidential information, ensure you keep it in a safe place. Having this report is especially beneficial for those of

SAMPLE HOUSEHOLD BUDGET REPORT
(Monthly)

SUMMARY	Budgeted	Actual		
Total income	$6,700.00			
Total expenses	$6,491.74			
Income less expenses	**$ 208.26**			
INCOME		Actual		
Wife's Salary	$2,000.00			
Husband's Salary	$3,400.00			
Rental Property	$1,300.00			
Total income	**$6,700.00**			
INVESTMENTS	Budgeted	Actual	Due Date	Status
IRA - Husband	$ 100.00		1st	
IRA - Wife	$ 100.00		1st	
Child's 529 Fund	$ 50.00		15th	
Child's 529 Fund	$ 50.00		15th	
Household Money Market Acct	$ 100.00		15th	
Total withholdings	$ 400.00			
Percent of expenses	**6.16%**			

you who travel often or have very busy lives. It makes it easy to pay your bills and track what activity has occurred. Once you have used this method for about six months, spend some time reviewing your progress. What adjustments can be made to save or curtail spending? It is a simpler way to monitor your financial status with fewer headaches as compared to some other more expensive options available where software packages are sold. Remember, the focus to becoming more financially savvy is to do more with less.

As you evaluate your operations expenses, I am sure some things were not a surprise to you. However, you probably learned how much

SAMPLE HOUSEHOLD BUDGET REPORT
(Monthly)

FINANCE PAYMENTS	Budgeted	Actual	Due Date	Notes
Capital One	$ 75.00		1st	
Auto loan Vehicle 1	$ 543.00		1st	123-456-7890
				Acct#1234567
MBNA	$ 60.00		15th	
Auto loan Vehicle 2	$ 420.92		1st	
Mortgage (Rental)	$ 993.10		1st	
Mortgage	$1,300.00		1st	
Total finance payments	$3,392.02			
Percent of expenses	*52.25%*			

HOUSEHOLD EXPENSES	Budgeted	Actual	Due Date	Notes
Lawn Service	$ 140.00			
Charitable donations	$ 335.00		1st & 15th	
Auto insurance	$ 135.00		1st	
Children's Tuition	$ 700.00		1st & 15th	
Water and Sewer	$ 30.00		10th	
Cellphone	$ 81.00		15th	
Life Insurance	$ 77.72		1st	
Cable TV	$ 51.00		15th	
Telephone / DSL	$ 130.00		1st	
Electric	$ 120.00		1st	
Total household expenses	$1,799.72			
Percent of expenses	*27.72%*			

VARIABLE EXPENSES	Budgeted	Actual	Due Date	Notes
Household				
Groceries	$ 200.00			50 weekly
Auto upkeep and gas	$ 180.00			Both vehicles
			45 weekly	
Other travel expenses				
Furniture				
Clothing				
Hair/Nails	$ 120.00			
Medical/prescriptions				
Husband's Allowance	$ 200.00			50 weekly -
Wife's Allowance	$ 200.00			50 weekly -
Other				
Total variable expenses	**$ 900.00**			
Percent of expenses	*13.86%*			

those decisions are impacting your financial portfolio. It is hard to ignore what is staring at you in black and white. No more thoughts of out of sight, out of mind. We have to deal with those items of discomfort and make an effort to improve our position. One thing is for sure, you are not the only person in this situation so you are not alone. However, you are the only one who can improve your personal situation. With that said, let's get to it! Let us discuss the subject of the plastic wonder ticket called a credit card.

Credit Cards

There are advantages to having the plastic wonder ticket to purchasing power. Credit cards have many benefits to the consumer. The two key advantages to having a credit card are to build your credit and to handle emergency situations. Having a favorable credit score will help you purchase the needs for life survival such as a home or a car. Consider these suggestions to building your credit.

- If you are just starting out with a credit card, make reasonable purchases that you can pay off each month. It is a good idea to have no more than two cards.

- You will start to receive other offers with varying incentives. The important ones are low interest rates and no membership fees. If the interest rates are three or more points lower, give up the higher rated card and close the account.

- Keep credit cards that have history. Do not close them but use them for emergency purposes only.

- If you have had the card for awhile, do not close the account. It may be the only history you have established.

The second advantage of having a credit card is for emergency situations. What constitutes an emergency purchase? It is not that suit or sofa you have been eyeing that just went on sale. An emergency situation worthy of charging is car repairs, an airline ticket for a funeral or sick relative and house repairs. (The things that you must have taken care of to maintain your needs.) The fact that you had to use the card indicates that you could not afford to pay for the expense completely upfront. Once you have completed the corrective actions, you must now put the focus on paying them off. Adjust your Household Report to accomplish that task.

We have all heard the saying "do not shop or spend to satisfy a want." I would recommend that if you have more than one credit card, take it out of your wallet. Leave one emergency card in your wallet for just that, an emergency! If you want it that badly, save for it. Something better is bound to come along later just as pretty and worthy of your purchase. Wait until you have saved the money for it. Remember, the goal is to be savvy, not to spend lavishly!

Purchasing a Home
One of the most important purchases you can ever make is a home. It has often been associated with being a part of the American dream. We have set the groundwork by preparing a budget, filing system and discussing the use of credit cards. Now you are prepared to consider this next step in being financially savvy. Consider these suggestions as you apply and prepare for purchasing a home:

• Don't use your credit cards a few months before applying.

• Review your credit report. Visit the following website to learn more about your credit score and obtain your report, www.myfico.com or www.privacyguard.com.

- Start writing a letter to explain any late payments or other negative activity.

- Do not apply for anything that will require an inquiry on your report.

- Pay off credit cards months before you plan to apply but do not close accounts.

- Review your last three bank statements. Are there areas of concern? Address them now.

- How much house do you *need*, not *want*?

- Save for your down payment.

- Research the area where you are considering your home purchase for cost effectiveness.

- Get an estimate on the property taxes.

- Get an estimate on the insurance premium.

- Pay to have a house inspector representing you determine the condition of the home.

- Purchase a home warranty after the first year if the home is not new.

  (It could save you money and headaches in the long run.) Most home repairs are covered by the warranty.

Building Wealth and Retirement Preparation

The information provided so far has discussed how to build credit or position yourself for financial success. Now that you have the framework, how do you go about increasing your financial stability? There are several ways to accomplish this task. Let's take a look at some strategies.

- Focus on a career promotion.

- Take on a part-time job.

- Participate in investment opportunities.

- Turn a hobby or interest into a small business.

Career Promotion and Part-time Jobs

A career promotion would bring in a larger salary. What we as women would need to do to become financially savvy in the workplace requires skill in negotiations. Often times we, as women, accept the salary being offered without challenging the employer to give more. It is no secret that men make more than women. How do we bridge the gap? Knowing how to play the deal-making game would help align you with your financial goals. Here are some ideas to consider:

- Is it a cause worthy of making a deal? A salary increase may not be as beneficial as time off. Know what you are willing to take as a substitute to receiving more money.

- You need to be able to provide benefits for your request.

- Have a strategic plan. You should not enter into discussion without careful thought. Be prepared for the discussion and the plan of action to occur if your efforts are successful or not.

- Listen intensely and ask what the employer or manager would like to achieve during the discussion.

- Consult with a mentor or career coach for more specific strategies.

Part-time employment also provides additional income. There are some things to be considered with this option as well. Discuss this with your family or determine how this will impact the rest of your life. Is it worth the additional money you will be making? Have a plan for using the extra money and how long it will take to achieve that goal. Plan your time carefully to include sufficient rest to perform your "bread and butter" position. With a plan you are in a better position to achieve your goals.

Before you take the plunge and start the job hunt, consider your current place of employment. It may not be a good idea to let your manager or members of your team know you will be working a second job. Only you know how this could affect your career. More importantly, revisit your company policy on customer or outside affiliation with other companies before applying for a position elsewhere. Lastly, you need to determine if you will have the flexibility needed to leave and go to another employer. Oftentimes there is not a hard stop time at work. You do not want to increase your stress level and affect your health in a negative way while trying to juggle the two opportunities.

Investing

Another way to build wealth is letting your money work for you. Take advantage of investment opportunities. Start with your current employer. Participate in 401(k) plans and stock options. Most 401(k) plans involve employer contributions along with your personal investment into the savings opportunity. Take advantage of the free money given to you. It is another benefit from your employer that you should take advantage of during your career. The other option available is investing into a Roth IRA. This individual retirement plan (IRA) requires you to make monthly, quarterly or annual contributions to a fund that grows.

Do not hesitate to get a financial advisor. You need to sit down with an expert that can help you determine the best options for your individual situation. Most large companies offer discounts, even rebates, to employees to visit financial planning organizations. Check with your employer's benefits website or call human resources to find out if they participate or suggest options. If this option is not available, educate yourself by visiting financial websites, reading self-help books or asking your tax preparer for assistance.

The final way to build personal wealth is by utilizing your hobbies or interest in starting a small business. It requires more time and preparation than getting a second job. However, it could also lead to a career change or a self-sustaining venue for building wealth. More importantly, doing something that you enjoy can also be an emotional deposit into your well-being. You could bring in additional income to build your savings or pay off debt.

• Attend a small business start-up seminar.

• Consult with your tax advisor to ensure it will help with your financial goals.

• Spend time with a small business owner to learn the pros and cons.

• Find a local small business center for more information.

A key to building wealth is having multiple streams of income. The options mentioned to obtain extra money can be used to reduce debt or build an emergency fund. Yes, this is one more thing to consider in your financial plan. It is recommended that once you have reduced your debt and built your wealth that you establish an emergency fund. This fund is one that you would use for those unexpected expenses that arrive. Previously we discussed using a credit card. Now you should use your emergency fund. It can also prepare you for survival in the event you should lose your job. This fund should be six months of your current salary. The quicker you reach your goals the more comfortable you can be at enjoying life. Spend the time now so that you can enjoy retirement and the finer things in life.

Law of Reciprocity

The success of your finances also depends on you reaching outside of your immediate arena. You are not in the world alone. You have made a conscious effort to better your conditions or you would not be reading this book. Others may not have gotten to the point where you have found yourself or require a little nudge. Let us take a look at how we can do that.

Give Back

Make a deposit in others. Help someone less fortunate. Stop putting the focus on yourself. Financial freedom or responsibility will affect more than just you. Some of us already have a family or plan to have one in the future. Preparation should begin now because it is never too early or too late. Give and it will be given back to you. It may not be in the same method but you want to ensure you are sowing good seeds. Consider these suggestions:

- Give what you can afford to give. The level of your gift should be comfortable with your pocketbook as well as your consciousness.

- Giving is not just a financial decision. You can give of your time and talents.

- Reach back and educate the next generations on financial lessons you have learned.

Tithes or Spiritual Affiliation

This level of giving back is very personal. It depends on your religious preference and belief. Many of you pay tithes (which is ten percent of your income) to your house of faith. Again, money is not the only way you can accomplish generosity. Spend time helping others. You will see how fortunate you are in your life and areas you need to improve for continued success. Just think how much you have gained because someone else was willing to deposit into your life.

Success does not come from flying solo throughout your life. Everyone needs someone for survival. Take the time, money, lessons learned and your skills to help move someone else to the next level of becoming financially savvy. How can you do that? Consider these ideas:

• Contribute to your siblings, younger family members, friends or an adopted child's saving fund.

• Give to a mission supporting causes that are important to your beliefs.

• Search your home for items that you have not used in a while or you no longer need. If it is in good condition, it will be an asset to someone else.

A Little Extra

The discussion of becoming financially savvy has consisted of the not-so-popular responsibilities of improving your finances. I would like to conclude with ways you can treat yourself without breaking the Household Report. Yes, what we can do to build our emotions and pamper ourselves.

• Visit a school of massage for an inexpensive massage or facial rather than a luxurious day spa or resort until you can afford it.

• Treat yourself to a special dinner. Instead of going out, print out a recipe of your favorite dish or new dish the night before. Stop by the grocery store on the way home and purchase the items you need. Have dinner by candlelight and complement with a glass of wine.

• Turn your bathroom into a spa retreat. Take a trip to a Bath & Body Works, the Body Shop or any department store that carries bathroom essentials. You may spend $60 now but you can have at least one month of once-a-week getaways by not leaving your home. Pull out your basket of goodies for an hour of pampering.

• Consider visiting the hair salon less. Reconsider high maintenance looks that have the potential to cause a severe impact on your budget.

• Take advantage of customer award programs offered by companies. Utilize skymiles or hotel points earned from personal and/or business travel. Once you qualify for the hotel stay and airfare toward a vacation, the only expenses you will probably incur are meals.

• Obtain a new look to an older outfit. Consider buying accessories for what you already have instead of buying a new suit or dress. If it is in your budget or does not take away from your plan, buy a new blouse, sweater, scarf or belt.

You have now been equipped with tools and strategies to further position yourself for financial success. One thing you should keep in mind is that no one has mastered financial stability without lessons being learned. Revisit what you have been doing, implement the Household Budget Report and adjust your actions accordingly. Your happiness should not be measured by what you obtain. Instead become financially savvy and take control of your finances.

Financial Quiz

You left college with a degree, student loans and credit card debt. What should you do to be come financially savvy?

Solution: Consolidate your student loan to the lowest interest rate. Because the rate on your loan is usually lower than your credit cards, see if you can defer it for a year. Focus on your highest interest rated cards and pay them off first. Close them once they are paid off especially if they are department store cards and will you not need the credit history for a future home purchase. You will want to keep a credit card for emergencies. You can now put funds toward your student loans.

Resources

Read Suze Orman's book, *The Money Book for the Young, Fabulous & Broke.* visit www.suzeorman.com.

For credit card debt assistance: www.bankrate.com.

For retirement preparation, visit www.smartmoney.com/retirement.

To determine your FICO score, visit www.myfico.com or www.privacy guard.com.

ABOUT THE AUTHOR

SHARVA HAMPTON-CAMPBELL

Sharva Hampton-Campbell, a native of Louisiana, resides in Champaign, Illinois with her husband, Marshall, and her mother, Patricia. She received a Bachelor's and Master's degree in Social Work from the University of Illinois at Champaign–Urbana. Ms. Hampton-Campbell also completed paralegal training at Roosevelt University and conflict resolution and mediation training from Aurora University in Chicago, Illinois. She is employed full-time as an academic advisor at Parkland College and is an independent social work consultant and counselor. Currently, Ms. Hampton-Campbell is working on her clinical social work license.

Ms. Hampton-Campbell provides staff development training and workshops for public and private social service agencies, as well as youth seminars for churches and community based youth organizations. She has developed and conducted the following workshops: "Becoming a Competent Case Manager," "It's all About the Attitude," "Engaging African American Youth: A Strength's Perspective," and "Show Me the Money: Financial Planning for Teens." She is also a Certified Trainer on women's issues, diversity and multiculturalism, and youth issues. Her latest projects are the development of Sista Circle, a Christian youth program that focuses on studying the word of God, giving back to the community and academic excellence, as well as Youth Empowered for Success (Y.E.S.), a therapeutic mentoring program for youth aged 11 to 18 years old.

Ms. Hampton-Campbell is a member of The Professional Woman Network International Advisory Board, and has received national recognition in *Who's Who Among America's Teachers.*

Contact:
Sharva Hampton-Campbell
P.O. Box 135
Champaign, IL 61824
(217) 202-5498
shamcamp@hotmail.com
www.protrain.net

FIVE

OVERCOMING OBSTACLES

By Sharva Hampton-Campbell

I can do all things through God who strengthenth me. Phil 4:13 (KJV)

Webster's dictionary defines obstacles as "things that stand in the way; hindrances or obstructions." What is your definition of obstacles? I believe obstacles are things we allow to get in the way of our progress, our progress forward, our reaching of new heights...etc. I have referred to them as stumbling blocks on many occasions. Obstacles come in the form of fear, anxiety, nervousness, disappointment, intimidation, humiliation, and criticism. They also stem from poor choices. "Murphy's Law" has also been the blame for a lot of obstacles as well. Several close friends, who are established professionals, have identified promotions and demotions as obstacles that hindered their careers early on. In your quest to become a professional woman you will be faced with many obstacles, some of which I have listed above and others that will present themselves in a totally different manner.

This is what I call a "think and do" chapter. It is filled with thought-provoking exercises that will help you to assess your ability to overcome obstacles. I will share personal examples that I hope will enlighten you and give you some encouragement as you pursue your career goal(s). Earlier I posed the question "What is your definition of obstacles?" Please take a minute and provide your definition below.

EXERCISE 1

My definition of obstacles is:

_____

_____

_____

Now that you have conceptualized a term that has some very negative connotations, I would like you to do some brainstorming about how to overcome the very thing(s) you listed in your definition.

EXERCISE 2

List as many words as you can in response to the following statements:

1. Examples of obstacles are:

_____

_____

_____

2. To overcome means to:

_____

_____

_____

3. Skills and characteristics necessary to overcome are:

_____

_____

_____

I now want you to place a check mark by each of the skills and characteristics that you possess. Put a star by the ones that you want to develop. (When I completed this exercise I realized I had more skills and characteristics that impacted my ability to overcome than I had given myself credit for. I began to reminisce and replay in my mind major obstacles that I had experienced and how I overcame them or allowed them to hinder my progress.) The next exercise will give you the opportunity to do the same.

EXERCISE 3
On a separate sheet of paper or in your journal, write about the following:

1. Describe any obstacles that you overcame and explain how you overcame each of them.

2. Identify your feelings connected to overcoming each obstacle.

3. Describe any obstacles that have hindered your progress forward and the barriers that have kept you from overcoming them.

4. Identify your feelings connected to each obstacle.

Now that you have had the opportunity to review your personal experience with handling obstacles, how would you rate your ability to overcome?
Scale: 1= poor   10= excellent

If you rated yourself 4 or less, keep reading and don't skip any of the exercises. If you rated yourself between 5 and 9, keep reading and complete the exercises that you feel are beneficial.

If you rated yourself a 10, please share the information presented in this chapter with someone you know who really wants to take a closer look at her ability to overcome life's challenges.

I firmly believe we all have an innate ability to overcome adversity. This is often referred to as resilience. Resilience is a person's ability to cope in the time of trouble. It also means you are able to "bounce back" after the experience is over and you learned something from the experience. Your ability to cope and regain composure is connected to external and internal drives such as personal connections and your sense of purpose. For some it is easy to tap into these mechanisms, but for others it is the most difficult thing to do. You might ask why this is so. Simple. Some of us are aware of these strengths and have relied upon them previously during times of need and others are not aware of them or don't believe they exist.

There are many factors that affect our level of resilience or ability to cope. The following list is not exhaustive but I believe has the greatest impact on our ability to cope.

Factors of Resilience
- Having family and friends who care about you and believe in you,
- Working in an environment where you feel appreciated and have a sense of belonging,
- Involving yourself in community-based organizations,
- Having a spiritual connection,
- Having a clear sense of your purpose in life,
- Having a strong belief in yourself, and
- Engaging in hobbies and activities for the sole purpose of enjoyment.

I have developed a questionnaire that relates to these factors. Complete the following exercise, as it will give you a closer look at your external and internal drives. External drives are people, places or things that impact you in some way. Internal drives are your emotions and feelings, ideas and thought processes. There is a direct correlation between the two. Your external drive affects your internal drives and both can drastically impact your ability to deal with life's challenges.

EXERCISE 4

Answer the following questions. Each answer is worth a certain number of points. At the end of the exercise use the chart to add your points and determine how your external and internal drives influence your coping skills.

1. Are your family and friends available during your time of need?
   Yes, always (a)   Sometimes (b)   No (c)   Not applicable (d)

2. Do your family and friends believe in you?
   Yes, always (a)   Sometimes (b)   No (c)   Not applicable (d)

3. Do you feel appreciated at work?
   Yes, always (a)   Sometimes (b)   No (c)   Not applicable (d)

4. If you are affiliated with any community-based organizations, do you feel a sense of belonging?
   Yes, always (a)   Sometimes (b)   No (c)   Not applicable (d)

5. If you are affiliated with a religious group, do you feel a sense of purpose?
   Yes, always (a)   Sometimes (b)   No (c)   Not applicable (d)

6. Do you believe in yourself?
   Yes, always (a)   Sometimes (b)   No (c)   Not applicable (d)

7. Do you spend quality time doing something that you enjoy?
   Yes, always (a)   Sometimes (b)   No (c)   Not applicable (d)

8. Do you allow your family and friends to take advantage of you?
   Yes, always (a)   Sometimes (b)   No (c)   Not applicable (d)

9. Do you allow others to take advantage of you?
   Yes, always (a)   Sometimes (b)   No (c)   Not applicable (d)

10. Are you easy to get along with?
    Yes, always (a)   Sometimes (b)   No (c)   Not applicable (d)

11. Do you act on impulse?
    Yes, always (a)   Sometimes (b)   No (c)   Not applicable (d)

12. Do you think things through before you act or react?
    Yes, always (a)   Sometimes (b)   No (c)   Not applicable (d)

13. Are you able to adjust to change?
    Yes, always (a)   Sometimes (b)   No (c)   Not applicable (d)

14. Do you have a sense of humor?
    Yes, always (a)   Sometimes (b)   No (c)   Not applicable (d)

15. Do you use your talents?
    Yes, always (a)   Sometimes (b)   No (c)   Not applicable (d)

Add your points:

Quantity of each letter x points per letter
a _____ x 5 = _____
b_____ x 3 = _____
c_____ x 1 = _____
d_____ x 0 = _____

Total points = _____

The total possible points you can score is 75. Mark your score on the graph below.

```
0      10     20     30     40      50      60     70  75
L_____I_____I_____I_____I_____I_____I_____I___J
```

I grew up in rural Louisiana. My family was a part of the working-poor. My mother was a single parent who worked as many jobs as she had to in order to meet our basic needs (i.e., food, shelter and clothing). She oftentimes left my brother and me in the care of my great-aunt for months at a time to seek employment opportunities out of town, even out of state. I admired her for her determination and perseverance to provide for her family. This was a commonality among the women on the maternal side of my family. I observed the presence of these traits every time they were faced with adversities.

My mother's strong willpower and tenacity influenced my development of coping skills. Also, my great-aunt's gentleness impacted my ability to cope with misfortunes. Her uncanny wisdom and kind words were very soothing to my pre-adolescent development, no matter how distraught I was over losing my allowance or skinning my knee. She taught me to assess the situation by determining the possible outcomes, then decide which outcome was the most feasible to accomplish. For example, when I lost my allowance, I applied her principle. I assessed the situation and determined the possible outcomes were: I could live with the fact that I wouldn't get another allowance for two weeks; I could ask for an advance; or I could ask if there were any opportunities to earn some extra money (i.e., doing extra chores, running errands, etc). I chose the latter and was able to earn back what I had lost. I still apply this principle today in my everyday living as well as in my profession when I am faced with obstacles. There are some strong-willed women in my family who impacted my ability to cope. The following exercise will help you identify the external factors that have impacted your ability to cope.

EXERCISE 5

On a separate sheet of paper or in your journal, answer the following questions.

1. Who was instrumental in developing your ability to cope?

2. How did they impact your life?

3. Are they aware of the positive impact they had on your personal development?

If yes, I hope they are still actively involved in your life. If no, I challenge you to share this vital information with them, if it is feasible to do so.

I would like to introduce you to Yalanda, a successful attorney. She and I met in college. We shared many stories about our upbringing. She has agreed to share her story of the people who impacted her ability to cope.

Yalanda's Story

"When I was a teenager my grandmother told my cousin and me (who was two years older than I) that we would "never amount to anything." She told us we would engage in unhealthy relationships and we would bear children from each of these relationships. My grandmother called us lazy, trifling, irresponsible and worthless. I was taught always to respect my elders so I never responded verbally to my grandmother's comments. I constantly replayed her words in my head, especially when my life seemed to be falling apart. I used my grandmother's negative comments to motivate myself to pick up the pieces and move on because I had to prove to her that I would amount to something. I am now a successful lawyer but my cousin unfortunately travelled down the road my grandmother paved with her negative words of discouragement."

When Yalanda first told me this story I could identify with her strong resolve and desire (internal drives) to prove herself. I had a similar experience in high school. During my senior year, my guidance counselor told me that I was not "college material" because I had taken more career-oriented courses (cooking, sewing, typing and shorthand) instead of college prep courses (advanced math and science). She suggested that I attend the local vocational center. I had dreams and aspirations of being a counselor and I knew that I would be selling myself short if I settled for vocational training. I told her in the most polite tone that I was going to cook, sew and go to college. I was appalled at the fact that she never asked me what my goals and aspirations were. She advised me based on assumptions. I also constantly replayed the conversation with my guidance counselor in my mind during my years in college, especially when I was overwhelmed with exams and research papers. My guidance counselor (external factor) inversely affected my determination (internal factor) to complete my undergraduate and graduate degrees and become a counselor. Can you identify the internal factors that have positively and negatively impacted your ability to cope? Let's refer to these as personal strengths and weaknesses.

EXERCISE 6
List 10 personal strengths and weaknesses and rank them, with 10 being the most significant and 1, the least significant.

Strengths   Rank

_____   _____

_____   _____

_____   _____

_____   _____

_____   _____

_____   _____

	Rank
_____	____
_____	____
_____	____

Weaknesses   Rank

_____	____
_____	____
_____	____
_____	____
_____	____
_____	____
_____	____
_____	____

Look at your top five weaknesses; can you turn those into strengths? Yes or No. If yes, how (what has to happen)?

_____

_____

_____

If no, are you okay knowing that you don't have the power or capacity to turn them into strengths?

_____

_____

Becoming a professional woman will not be an easy task; generally speaking, life is not filled with easy tasks. My mother has always told me, "Anything worth having is worth working for. If you want it badly enough you'll work hard enough!" Is the career you have in mind worth working hard for? How badly do you want it? More specifically, let's take a look at you and your career goals, dreams and aspirations.

EXERCISE 7

1. Who are you?

_____

_____

_____

2. What do you want out of life?

_____

_____

_____

3. What will it take to get there?

_____

_____

_____

4. What type of career do you want to embark upon?

_____

_____

_____

5. What will it take to gain entry into this particular field?

_____

_____

_____

6. What type of barriers are you up against?

_____

_____

_____

The information and exercises presented in this chapter should have helped you gain a better understanding of what it takes to overcome obstacles. I challenge you to map out your plan for Becoming the Professional Woman and proceed forward!

ABOUT THE AUTHOR

RIKI F. LOVEJOY-BLAYLOCK

Riki F. Lovejoy-Blaylock started receiving her own experience of working in a non-traditional environment when she entered the construction industry in 1985. Additionally, throughout her career, Riki has participated in college panel discussions and high school career days geared to encouraging women to choose non-traditional careers. Riki has been very active in the National Association of Women In Construction (NAWIC).

Riki has worked for major general contractors in the Orlando, Florida, market as a project manager and owned a carpentry subcontracting company in the early '90s. Additionally, she has worked on construction projects in Beijing, China and the Caribbean. Currently Riki is the Executive Director for RFL Consulting Solutions, LLC, a construction management consulting firm with management contracts on projects throughout the country.

Riki is also the Executive Director for Breaking the Barriers, providing seminars and workshops that address diverse corporate cultures and non-traditional career issues.

Riki has a B.S. in Business Management with a minor in Management Information Systems, is a certified Minority Business Enterprise through the Florida and Kentucky Minority Suppliers Development Council, as well as a certified Woman's Business Enterprise through the National Women Business Owners Corporation. In 2003–2004 Riki was named to Empire's *Who's Who of Business and Professional Executives.*

Contact:
RFL Consulting Solutions, LLC
(407) 443-3423
rlovejoy@rfl-consulting.com
www.rfl-consulting.com
www.protrain.net

SIX

WORKING IN A NON-TRADITIONAL WORK ENVIRONMENT

By Riki F. Lovejoy-Blaylock

Since the beginning of the 21st century, the term 'non-traditional career' has been one of the many new buzz words of the workforce world, especially as relates to women in the workforce. But what actually defines a non-traditional career?

According to the Department of Labor (DOL), Women's Bureau, a non-traditional occupation for women is one in which women comprise 25 percent or less of the total employment—and the list is pretty long, covering all major occupational groups.

Of course, the full 2003 list is much more extensive than is represented here. Interestingly enough, some occupations have actually dropped off the non-traditional occupations list, just since 1999, such as photographers, postal service mail carriers, lawyers and even physicians. More have been added like chefs/head cooks (19.4% in 2003),

NON-TRADITIONAL OCCUPATIONS FOR WOMEN IN 2003			
(Employment in thousands)			
Occupation	Employed Both Sexes	Employed Female	Percent Female
Upholsterers	56	14	25
Farmers and ranchers	825	204	24.7
Dishwashers	294	70	23.8
Baggage porters, bellhops & concierges	85	17	20
Computer hardware engineers	99	10	10.1
Refuse & recyclable material collectors	63	5	7.9
Electrical and electronic engineers	363	26	7.2
Misc. construction & related workers	58	4	6.9
Heating, air conditioning, refrigeration mechanics and installers	350	2	.6

Source: Excerpted from U.S. Department of Labor, Bureau of Labor Statistics, Non–traditional Occupations for Women in 2003.

aerospace engineers (11%), crane tower operators (3.3%) and roofers (1.3%). So why a non-traditional career? Non-traditional occupations offer women expanded opportunities for:

• Challenges/Diversity: It's rarely boring working in 'a man's world'!

• Pay scales: Typically non-traditional occupations have higher entry-level wages as well as better benefits both of which will offer a quicker path to economic independence.

• Career opportunities: Working 'up the ladder' offers continuous challenges, more diversity and even higher pay scales!

No matter the career choice, it takes more than just the money to stay passionate about your work, but let's face it, without the money, we cannot indulge our passions. So let's take a look at pay scales.

20 LEADING OCCUPATIONS OF EMPLOYED WOMEN			
Full-time Wage and Salary Workers 2003 Annual Averages *(Employment in thousands)*			
Occupation	Total Employed Women	Total Employed (Men and Women)	Percent Women	Women's Median Weekly Earnings
Total, 16 years and older (all employed women, full-time wage and salary workers)	44,076	100,302	43.9	$552
Secretaries and administrative assistants	2,692	2,794	96.3	$531
Elementary and middle school teachers	1,780	2,208	80.6	$757
Registered nurses	1,650	1,829	90.2	$887
Nursing, psychiatric, and home health aides	1,144	1,285	89	$372
Cashiers	1,040	1,378	75.5	$315
Customer service representatives	1,038	1,503	69.1	$503
First-line supervisors/managers of office and administrative support	984	1,450	67.9	$609
First-line supervisors/managers of retail sales workers	938	2,259	41.5	$496
Bookkeeping, accounting, and auditing clerks	894	978	91.4	$512
Receptionists and information clerks	831	892	93.2	$446
Accountants and auditors	784	1,344	58.3	$756
Retail salespersons	765	1,840	41.6	$382
Maids and housekeeping cleaners	682	806	84.6	$317
Secondary school teachers	540	1,009	53.5	$824
Waiters and waitresses	528	775	68.1	$318
Teacher assistants	527	580	90.9	$344
Office clerks, general	511	610	83.8	$502
Financial managers	491	952	51.6	$823
Preschool and kindergarten teachers	476	484	98.3	$493
Cooks	452	1,149	39.3	$317

Source: U.S. Department of Labor, Bureau of Labor Statistics, Annual Averages 2003.

According to the U. S. Department of Labor, Bureau of Labor Statistics the Women's Median Weekly Earnings was $552.

Conversely, the DOL also reports the seven occupations with the highest median weekly earnings among women who worked full-time in 2003 were ...

Lawyers–$1,413

Pharmacists–$1,364

Computer and information systems managers–$1,280

Chief executives–$1,243

Computer software engineers–$1,005

Physicians and surgeons–$989

Management analysts–$977

...all of which have been or are currently considered non-traditional careers for women. Even at the entry-level of industries such as construction, the national mean, full-time, hourly earning is $13.59 (approximately $543 weekly) according to the *National Compensation Survey: Occupations Wages in the United States, July 2003,* published by the U. S. Department of Labor, Bureau of Labor Statistics, August 2004. I don't know about you, but I do better with $543 per week than $206, the annual weekly salary based on the current $5.15 minimum wage!

At this point many of you are saying to yourselves that certain jobs are "men's work" and other jobs are "women's work." If you are saying this, it is because through most of your life your teachers, your family and your peers have pointed you toward this myth. While many of the occupations may need more 'brawn' than brain they are still not gender specific. Women of the 21st century have the brawn and the brains and CAN really do anything!

Okay, now you have some of the facts and figures (there's so much more out there!) and you have the arguments to share with your friends and family. You have decided to take that step toward training and education for a non-traditional career! Good for you! But what really happens now? What is the environment like for a young woman to enter a non-traditional career? The short, easy answer? It's not all roses; in fact, it is oftentimes downright nasty!

As in all career choices, we hope you have chosen one that you are passionate about—especially if you have chosen a non-traditional career! To become successful in whatever career choice you make, you will invest a lot of yourself in time, money, sweat and frustration to 'make it'! Make sure you are ready to do 'whatever it takes' by first being passionate about your choices.

In choosing a non-traditional occupation you need to be aware of the additional challenges you will face as you continue your career growth. I believe the first and foremost challenge (and really, this is a struggle) is the perception of who and what you are by your peers (which, remember will be mostly men)! Until you prove yourself to 'the guys', and you will have to constantly do so, the perception will be that you cannot perform the job, whether for lack of brawn or lack of brain, to the expectation of those men! A female aerospace engineer 'does not have the mathematic and/or scientific mind' to successfully put a rocket into space. A female roofer 'does not have the strength' to stock the roofs with those heavy shingles. Of course she does!

Then there is the question about sexual orientation. This struggle will be on-going even as you continue to prove yourself to your supervisors, your co-workers and your friends and family—because there will always be someone new to have to prove yourself. You will always be striving to be 'one of the boys.' This leads to our next challenge.

And that next challenge you will encounter is one of remembering who YOU are—a struggle of self. You will tend to lose your femininity (where are the makeup, the 'girly' accessories, the prim and proper manners?), and many days you will feel you have lost 'the softer side' of being a woman, the person you are. You will have to develop a thick-skinned attitude as you continue the daily battle of proving to your peers (remember all those men?!) your skill or ability in this non-traditional occupation. By now you are asking yourself what is she actually talking about here?

Remember the first challenge, that of fitting in or becoming 'one of the boys.' Of course, depending on which non-traditional occupation you choose, "fitting in" will be a custom-designed process. But maybe I can better explain this better using myself as an example.

I chose my non-traditional career—general construction—at the ripe old age of 27! I had worked in a couple of other industries—hospitality and insurance—for about ten years and could not find satisfaction in anything I was doing. I had brief exposure to a masonry subcontracting business and found it fascinating. But at 27, after a series of not-so-good circumstances of life, I had to make some life choices and finally decide on what I wanted to be now that I was all grown up! As I pondered this very important decision, I realized that I had already tried so many different avenues, all of which were leading me to nowhere, EXCEPT—ooh, aah I really enjoyed that construction period of my life! I decided this is what I'm going to do!

Once the choice was made I did some research on what I thought I would need in the form of education, experience, etc. and I soon discovered that construction was a wide-open industry as there were so many choices. I was really going to have a difficult time selecting my career path. I did soon learn, though, that I needed to start at the bottom and so accepted a position as a receptionist in a large general contracting company. During my interview with the vice president of the potential new company, he asked me what I thought my goal would be with this company. Without hesitation, I told him I wanted to have his job.

I landed that receptionist position and once ensconced in my very important job, I realized I had a lot to learn to take over Mr. VP's job! In a five year period, I finished my two year degree in Construction Technology and moved up to a Project Manager position before the company officially closed its doors. However, once I moved out of the receptionist position (a typically "female" job), and moved into the men's turf it was a different world—even though I was still within that same company!

Toward the last year of the company's existence 'the new guy' was hired. He was fresh out of college with his 4-year degree and no experience. He got the job that should have actually been the next rung up for me—Project Engineer. At first I was okay with this slight because I convinced myself that he had the 4-year degree—mine was only two and I was still new to the industry. Well, the year rolled along and I taught 'the new guy' his job. Before his one year was up he got promoted to Project Manager! This time I got hot! Now I HAD to act like a man—forget those feminine ways—I was going to let the powers that be know in NO uncertain terms, I was very unhappy with this decision. It was a few more months, but I did get the promotion about five months before the company formally closed! Of course, my mindset was that it took 'the man in me' to make the difference! What (or more importantly who) was I becoming?

But with the closing of the company I decided to venture into— The Field! A co-worker (who also lost his job with the company closing) and I formed a partnership to be a carpentry subcontracting company. Trust me when I say, I had not ever really hammered a nail straight into a board in my life. Now I had a company that was so small (he and me!) that I had NO choice but to join him in the field. And I loved it! Carpenter-by-day, bookkeeper-legal advisor-President by night. But now working in the field was even more of a challenge than my first entry into the man's world. Now I had to have brawn and know-how (which IS different than brain in a man's mind)! Luckily, my partner had more faith in me than I did sometimes! But it definitely was very difficult to maintain any femininity in the field. But I always wore lipstick and earrings! I was not going to let these guys forget that I was a woman working in their manly world and doing a damn fine job! I also had to learn to keep my mouth and actions feminine. After a while though, I was actually accepted as one of the guys.

I found out about a year later that my business partner, who was actually in charge of hiring our crews, told every potential employee that first, "that woman was the boss" AND second, they would have to produce as much as I did on the project to keep their job and that was going to be THEIR challenge! This so amazed me that I did the only girlie thing I could do—I cried—which made me happy, too! I really thought I had made it in the man's world and I could still be a woman!

But the struggle continues with each new 'man's world' I enter. Working in the non-traditional environment means constantly having to prove your capabilities and, quite honestly, it doesn't matter at what level: Carpenter's helper, Project Engineer, President, Business Owner. The environment remains the same and you have to continue the struggle. But if you are passionate about the career choices you make, then this struggle just becomes another learning tool to becoming the consummate professional.

During this period of your life you may already be feeling quite overwhelmed as you make your career choices or continue your climb up the corporate ladder. So now you are probably asking yourself, "why would I want to add *these* challenges to my already confused life?" And here is your short, easy answer: it can be so much more rewarding in terms of challenges, diversity, pay scale, and career opportunities!

I touched on pay scale as a reward but how do challenges become a reward? If you are reading this book and this chapter has intrigued you even more, then you are a personality that needs 'challenges' to conquer to obtain fulfillment!

Working in the non-traditional environment offers plenty of other challenges besides those that come with entering a new industry or even those that I mentioned earlier in this chapter. The non-traditional environment offers opportunities for the welcomed challenge—those opportunities where you want to prove your own mettle. You may be the one to develop the new method or strategy that will save a project thousands of dollars or bring it in ahead of schedule. Or you will motivate a tense group of employees to the point of being the number one team! Whatever your contribution to your company, YOU will feel accomplished that you met and conquered whatever challenge crossed your path—including those of being in a non-traditional career environment. There's your reward and it's a big, fat one!

I have worked in the construction industry for twenty years! And I'm not going to bluff you to say I've loved every moment of it or that I have been passionate about what I'm doing at any given period, but I will tell you that I don't have regrets about the path I chose. I am an individual who needs to be in a constant state of learning. I have always, through the twenty years, continued to learn—whether it is about the industry, a new innovation within the industry or just how to flourish in a non-traditional career environment. And through it all, I have actually learned to be a professional. You, too, can become *The Professional Woman* in a non-traditional career.

Good Luck!

ABOUT THE AUTHOR

LINDA RISER

Linda Riser is a corporate etiquette, protocol and children's manners expert. As a speaker, teacher and advisor in the Southeast for more than twenty years, she is the Founder/Director of The Protocol School of Tennessee. She has received certification from Protocol School of Washington.

Ms. Riser is a leader, motivator and business owner. As co-owner of Riser Aviation and R&R Enterprises, she has taught radio communication to student pilots. Her teaching background includes adult literacy, etiquette, protocol, image and manners for children, professionalism and customer service.

Ms. Riser is a frequent contributor to trade and business publications, magazines, television and radio talk shows. She is active in professional and civic organizations and is a member of The Professional Woman Network International Advisory Board, International Association of Protocol Consultants, Livingston Airport Authority, Friends of the Overton County Library, and Volunteer Coordinator for the Livingston Bicentennial.

Linda Riser lives in Livingston, Tennessee with her husband Roy and Oats (the dog) in a 100-year-old historical home.

Contact:
The Protocol School of Tennessee
107 Court Square
Livingston, TN 38570
(931) 823-7357
lriser@twlakes.net
www.protrain.net

SEVEN

ETIQUETTE

By Linda Riser

What is etiquette? One definition is "rules governing socially acceptable behavior." An example of the use of etiquette from centuries ago can be shown through Louis XIV's gardener. When this servant discovered that the aristocrats were trampling through the gardens he had worked so hard to produce, he put up signs that read "Keep off the Grass," but many chose to ignore the requests and continued to tramp through the gardens. If we stay within the flexible bounds of etiquette, we will be able to present ourselves with confidence and authority in all areas of our professional lives. Etiquette includes knowing how to treat others with respect in all situations and putting people at ease when they are in our company. So in the next few minutes, I hope that you will be helped by the information that is presented to you in this section of *Becoming the Professional Woman*.

Let's begin with an example of an occasion when you have been invited to a business gathering. More than likely, you have been invited because your host feels like you will have something to contribute to this gathering. The last place you want to go is the food table. When you enter the room, pause at the door to see whom you might want to talk to. As you make your way around the room, you simply make small talk. I would advise that before you go to this gathering, if possible, find out who is going to be there by asking the host for a list of the guests. Mixing and mingling is a wonderful opportunity for networking and meeting people, business people and your colleagues. The beautiful thing here is that these gatherings are a blend of business and pleasure. Following a few minutes of visiting and making conversation, it is then permissible to go to the bar or the food table. Have something to eat, along with a beverage. I would suggest that you leave a space on your plate to set your drink. This type of gathering is for mingling with those who have also attended.

The CEO of your company may ask you to go as a representative and you want to make absolutely sure that you know how to present yourself with confidence and authority. It is no secret that persons who know the three Cs will be successful: That is *Competency, Confidence and Consideration of others.* Some good tips to remember are to read at least one daily newspaper and to read a weekly newspaper before going to an event, business or social. Be prepared to discuss these items of current events, books, films, and television shows. You want to steer clear of topics that might cause controversy.

Table Manners

Table manners aren't just for those in the business world. Every one of us can benefit from good manners. Before the meal even begins, males should remove hats and caps if they have been worn. After being seated at the table, placement of silverware should be noted. Don't pick up a utensil before your host is at the table, unless the host says, "Go ahead and start the meal." Then you are free to do so. We begin from the outside in, and if someone is uncertain about the placement of the bread plate, remember BMW: Bread, Meal and Water. Your napkin is to be picked up and lowered beneath the table, unfolded and placed on your lap.

Simple table setting ("map set") Bread, meal, water (BMW) placement.

Formal table setting

Knife and fork holding:

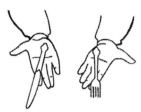
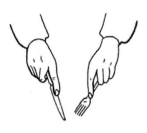

Incorrect ways of handling silverware:

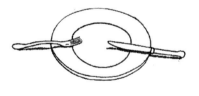

Two styles of eating are American Style and Continental Style. Whether it is a two-course, four-course or seven-course meal, you must always try just a little bit of everything that is served to you, unless you know that you are allergic to it. You do not say to your host, "I don't like that." You want to take a quick sip of water if a bite of food is too hot. Begin your meal by using your utensils from the *outside first.* Always take small bites and do not talk with your mouth full of food. If you must take medication, do it very discreetly. If you are diabetic and a daily

American style of holding knife and fork:

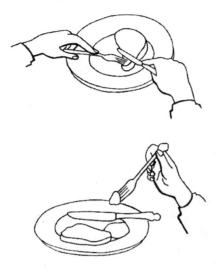

Continental style of holding knife and fork:

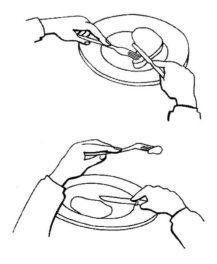

procedure is necessary, the bathroom is the more appropriate place to do this. Doing this at the table is totally unacceptable. Also, don't forget to place your napkin on your chair when you excuse yourself during a meal. Something else you don't want to do is to apply lipstick while dining. If you want to freshen up, excuse yourself and go to the bathroom. Do not sit there in front of your guests or the whole restaurant and put lipstick on. It is not appropriate. If you have a purse, especially a large one, set it on the floor next to your feet. It does not go on the table. If during a meal you should get a fishbone in your mouth, remove it with your forefinger and thumb and place it on the side of your plate. Do remember your posture at the table. You do not slump or put your elbows on the table. When you eat soup, think of a fish swimming out to sea. The spoon is dipped at the front of the bowl and lifted at the back. When you are finished with your meal, your utensils should be placed together at "4:30" on your plate. This indicates to the host/hostess or waiter that you are finished.

Dos and Don'ts for Professional Women

Right at the top of that list is gum chewing. If you are going to chew gum, get in your closet and close the door! Please do not go out in public chewing gum. Don't go into a restaurant chewing gum. If you happen to do that, discreetly put it in a tissue, put it in your purse, take it home with you, but do not put it on the side of your plate while you are eating your meal.

Some other guidelines in the professional business world that we will touch on include our behavior with fellow workers. Men and women always stand for introductions, whether it is in a business or social setting. When someone walks into your office, you want to make sure that you rise when you are introduced. The woman always extends her hand. Many years ago women did not shake hands very often, but that has changed. The only time that people do not stand when introduced is in a crowded situation.

If you are introducing people in a group where everyone is on a first-name basis, you would just say, "Mary Smith, I want to introduce Tom Jones" or in a more formal setting "Ms. Smith, I want to introduce Mr. Jones." You always add just a little bit of information about the person because this gives him/her a chance to get into a conversation. For instance, you would say, "Debbie Smith, I want to introduce John Hills. John and I were classmates in college and he is here on business." Say the new person's name and then give the name of the other persons in the group. If you can't remember all of the names, it is correct, acceptable and practical to say the new person's name and suggest that the other people introduce themselves.

Your handshake is important. You want to make sure that you have a firm handshake and that it is web-to-web, no bone crushing, no glove, and no patting someone on the shoulder. Some other office protocol we should remember: We do not drop into someone else's office unannounced. If someone comes into your office unannounced just to chat, stand up and move toward the door. This is a powerful sign that says, "I do not have time to talk with you right at the moment." Be friendly, firm and polite. When time is spent with co-workers, whatever you do, don't criticize your company. Don't complain about the problems. Don't complain about other co-workers or you might not get the promotion that you were hoping for. Do keep confidences, both personal and professional. Don't gossip and don't listen to gossip.

You will always want to reply to an invitation promptly. (I would also suggest that when hosting your own event, instead of putting "R.S.V.P." on the invitation that you put "Respond by" and put the date on there).

You want to make sure that you make the most of every event by planning ahead. You want to find out who is going to be there. Make sure that you ask. You want to learn to mingle. Mingle ability is just so important.

Body Language

Body language speaks volumes. Tons of research has been conducted and dozens of books written on the subject. The results of the studies in non-verbal communication have been substantiated over and over. Please remember that 55% of someone's impression of you is visual, 38% is presentation, and words account for only about 7% of the impact of your message. We communicate with our bodies. The less you rely on gestures, the more confidence and authority you will appear to have.

Telephone Etiquette

How do you sound on the telephone? Your appearance may be just fine, but how do you sound? Most of the business today is conducted over the telephone. Messages are conveyed through the words you use and through the vocal quality. Do you really listen to yourself when you talk? When answering the phone, you want to be pleasant. I suggest that you put a mirror close to your telephone and smile at yourself. Are you slumped over? If you are, your voice is going to sound like a frog. Sit up straight and before you answer the phone, take a deep breath. If you are going to take a message for someone, make sure you get it right. You always say, "Goodbye." Let the caller hang up first. When you hang up your telephone, do so gently. When you call someone, you want to be sure that you say your name i.e. "Hello. This is Helen Hughes calling for Mary Jones." When others call you, avoid the cliché of "Have a nice day." I think we have worn that out. If you need to put someone on a speaker phone, ask his or her permission. Don't just do it without the caller's knowledge because it may not be appreciated at all.

Corporate Culture

Harry Truman said, "Leadership is the ability to get men to do what they don't want to do and like it." A successful meeting is brief, focused and productive. The key to making it a success is planning. It is being considerate about the scheduling of a meeting. You want to know the participants. Most of the time, meetings are best held in the mornings. Friday afternoon is not a good time to have a meeting or the eve of a major holiday. You want to distribute the agenda well in advance of this meeting so people will know what will be discussed. You want to introduce or let people introduce themselves so everybody will know who is who and what department they are from. The person conducting the meeting should do so with tact, diplomacy and strength. Always start on time and end the meeting on time. Make sure that you thank the participants for giving their time, because it is their time.

The hierarchy of seating goes from left to right. The chairperson is to the immediate left of the person who has the most influence in the meeting. Be sure that you turn off your cell phone or mute it so this is not interrupted. The Japanese have taught us the importance of properly presenting and receiving business cards. On your business card you do not use Mr., Ms., or any honorific, unless your name could be construed as either masculine or feminine. In that case, use the honorific. For example, if your name is Johnnie Brown, use Ms. Johnnie Brown. That is permissible. Make sure your business cards are not dog-eared. When you hand people your business card, turn it facing them. You want to carry business cards at social events, in case a good business contact presents itself. Hand out your cards discreetly. Never produce a business card at a private luncheon or dinner (unless asked specifically by someone to do so). Do remember that you only have one opportunity to make a good, first impression. You don't get a second chance. Eye contact is very important and not reserved just for the first time. You want to make sure that you look directly into the eyes of the person that you are talking with. You want to maintain eye contact and don't overlook the impact of a smile because that is very important. Make sure that you use proper grammar because you can sabotage yourself really quickly. You want to avoid phrases such as, "You know?", "You see?", "You know what I mean?" You really want to avoid that.

The professional woman's business dress allows for more self-expression and individuality than men's attire because women have more choices and there is more room for error. Women are always challenged to project a professional, positive image, while expressing their own personality and taste. You do not want to make strong fashion statements, unless you are in the fashion business. Women are free to choose their professional attire. The suit will always be in vogue where a professional woman is concerned. If you look in your closet and all you see is navy or black, brown and taupe, be sure that you have wonderful accessories to brighten these colors up because in today's market, the professional woman can wear and use accessories such as pins and scarves.

Casual Friday

I do not believe that jeans are to be seen in a professional office, or when meeting with clients. Casual dress is not for a professional office. Most organizations probably do have a dress code, and it really should be enforced. Another thing to remember is that when you have a day off from work, don't leave home to run an errand or to go to the grocery store looking like you just crawled out of bed. You might run into business colleagues and clients, and you will be remembered by how you look.

Afternoon Tea

Afternoon tea is becoming the business meal. Executives are preferring this because of cost savings and because it is in the middle of the afternoon. Tea is less costly and alcohol is not served. Some upscale restaurants and hotels now serve afternoon tea, sandwiches and scones. You want to remember that the place of honor is always to the right of your host. Begin eating when your host picks up his/her fork. If you need to excuse yourself during the tea, just place your napkin on your chair. You do not put your napkin back on the table until the tea is finished.

I hope you've enjoyed these few minutes and that you have learned something to help you on the journey to becoming a person who always incorporates the rules that govern socially acceptable behavior. You'll find these valuable tools will make all the difference in how well you achieve your goals in the world of business.

Resources:

Protocol by Mary Jane McCaffree and Pauline Innis
The Little Book of Etiquette by Dorothea Johnson
Tea and Etiquette by Dorothea Johnson

Special thanks to the following:

Dorothea Johnson, Founder of The Protocol School of Washington, D.C.
Linda Eastman, CEO and Founder of The Professional Woman Network
Kim Emrich and Emily Sells
My Best Friend, Roy

ABOUT THE AUTHOR

BRENDA WARD, PH.D.

Brenda E. Ward, Ph.D., is Founder and President of Bren-Barr Associates, Inc., a Professional and Personal Development Education and Training Consulting Company, located in Long Island, New York. Her extensive professional experience spans twenty-five years. She is an accomplished education and training specialist, corporate executive, motivational leader and mentor.

Dr. Ward is an active member of The Professional Woman Network International Speakers Bureau and other professional organizations, including The International Third World Leaders Association. She is also active in voluntary community service in Nassau County, New York, and has written articles in various professional publications.

Her academic credentials include: Ph.D. in Health and Human Services, Post- Masters Certificate in Nursing Administration, Master of Arts in Community Health Education, Bachelor of Arts in Health Sciences, New York State Registered Professional Nurse License and certification as Diversity Educator and Youth Relations Trainer.

Dr. Ward has received numerous nursing professional, community service, and business awards.

Contact:
Brenda E. Ward, Ph.D
Bren-Barr Associates, Inc.
3280 Sunrise Highway, # 398,
Wantagh, NY 11793
(516) 221-6989
Brenbarr@optonline.net
www.Brenbarr.com
www.protrain.net

EIGHT

ASSERTIVENESS SKILLS

By Dr. Brenda Ward

Assertiveness is one of the most crucial attributes for success, although it is frequently misused, misunderstood and to some degree, often confused with aggressiveness. Understanding and practicing assertiveness to your fullest potential unleashes and exposes the critical element of self-power. The effective use of self-power is pivotal to achieving professional success.

Assertiveness may be defined in a variety of ways, such as:

• A mode of communication that is characterized by open and free expression of your thoughts and views in a manner that is pleasant and direct. These expressions may be verbal or non-verbal and are tempered with tact, sensitivity and respect for the opinion of others. The assertive individual is always aware of the potential for opposition.

• A reflection of your level of self-esteem and your ability to effectively advocate for yourself without compromising positive feelings or relationship.

- The optimum of positive mental health and is directly related to self-confidence, effective self-management and personal success.

Regardless of the definition you choose, recognize that assertiveness is an imperative for your success. It marshals and integrates the core dimensions of your person and gives a visible comprehensive picture of who you are. It defines the quality of your verbal communication, attitude, self-presentation, knowledge, and self-management ability. It embodies your total image, and your image is a benchmark by which you are judged. Your success, therefore, to a significant extent is predicated upon the impact that your image has upon others, which in turn determines how others respond to you.

The basic foundation for assertiveness is effective self-management, which emanates from a healthy perspective on life. It is an ongoing process that requires self-awareness, self-control, responsiveness, focus, knowledge of your potential, your personality and the importance of charting a course to achieve your value-based goals. It mandates that you understand that productivity is the quality and quantity produced, and is a core indicator of your level of self-management. Developing or refining your assertiveness skills is an adventure in self-discovery and self-empowerment.

Let us explore some principles of assertiveness within the framework of the critical dimensions of Communication, Attitude, Self-presentation, and Knowledge.

Dimensions

Becoming an Assertive Verbal Communicator

Your level of assertiveness manifests itself in your verbal communication in face-to-face encounters, writing, and in telephone conversations.

When you communicate:

• Recognize that your level of self-confidence and self-esteem dictates the quality of your communication. Therefore, the source of effective communication lies within you.

• Assess your level of self-confidence and self-esteem. Ask yourself these questions. How sure am I about my capabilities? To what degree do I love myself? The answer to these questions will help you to determine your parameters for any necessary adjustments.

• Be bold but not brash, professional but not haughty, and business-like but not dogmatic.

• Communicate with confidence and authority. Deliver your message clearly with energy and enthusiasm. It should be clear from your communication that you are knowledgeable, and your message and your audience are important.

• When speaking, do so at a moderate pace, in a low-pitched tone. Use good grammar and enunciate well. Pause but do not hesitate with, "uh, ah, um." Avoid using words that you have difficulty pronouncing.

• When starting conversations that involve giving a directive or making a request, never start with an apology or unnecessary preamble. Clearly and respectfully state your point. Instead of saying, "If you don't mind, please bring me the report," say, "Please bring me the report." This reflects assertiveness and leadership.

• Be a good listener. Listen with your eyes, ears and your posture. Keep your head up, face the audience or person and look directly at them. Demonstrate that you are attentive and focused and wait to interpret and respond to what you have heard. Never be too anxious and rush to respond as this will send a message that you are reactive rather than responsive.

- Always expect the unexpected and be prepared to respond in a composed, confident manner. If you allow unexpected or difficult situations to render you confused and ineffective you will be viewed as weak.

- Be calm, responsive and polite when dealing with difficult people and situations. Be like a duck in a pond: calm and smooth on the water's surface but feet working hard to maintain movement.

- Avoid engaging in self-sabotage. Always give yourself the benefit of the doubt. Do not make statements assuming that you are wrong. Instead of saying "I may be wrong, but I think that the room should be rearranged," say, "I think the room should be rearranged."

- Be comfortable saying "no." You have the right to do so if it is not a mandate or specific directive. However, say "no" respectfully, cordially and timely. Do not feel guilty. Keep your composure, and offer an alternative if possible. Say, "No I will not do the report for you but I will send you some information that will be helpful to you." This preserves the integrity of your relationship and reduces stress.

Remember, mastering the principles of assertive verbal communication can redefine who you are and garner you one of your greatest commodities for success, which is *trust*.

Projecting an Assertive Attitude

To develop and project an assertive attitude, you must understand the answers to these questions:

- What is attitude?
  Attitude is a response that gives visible evidence of your psychological image. Attitude may be positive and assertive or negative and aggressive.

- What is its source of origin and control?
  Contrary to some thinking, attitude is not hereditary, but is learned and is self-generated. The source of origin and the locus of control for your attitude is in your thoughts, beliefs and values. Pause and take a moment to go through this process.

Conjure up a thought and hold it in your mind. How does that thought make you feel? As a result of how you are feeling, what is the attitude that this feeling has generated? Positive and assertive or negative and aggressive? Based upon this attitude, what action or behavior are you most likely to engage in? You see, your thoughts have a powerful influence on the quality of your life.

What Does Attitude Do?

Your attitude reveals your overall mind-set, which is how you are thinking and it is a powerful indicator of how you feel about yourself, your work and others. It triggers behavior. Your attitude can make or break you in life. Assertiveness embodies a positive, responsive attitude and is a critical attribute to achieving professional success.

Here are some relative principles that will help you to develop or refine your assertiveness skills:

- Remember that your thoughts control your attitude. Therefore, take control of your thoughts and make positive thinking a habit.

- Engage in self-assessment so that you know your strengths, weaknesses and ability to influence others.

- Showcase your strengths selectively without flaunting.

- Willingly and readily take control of any situation, even if it means delegating tasks.

- Be open and receptive to feedback. Be confident and sensitive to the fact that not all feedback will be positive. Whenever you receive feedback, pleasantly say, "Thanks for sharing that." This reflects confidence and openness. Challenge respectfully and coherently.

- Give objective feedback with sensitivity to be constructive not destructive.

- Be comfortable saying, "I'm sorry" when you are wrong. This shows integrity and openness.

- Always view situations objectively, not emotionally. Never personalize them.

- Be responsive, not reactive. This shows that others, circumstances or events, are not controlling you.

- Be open and receptive to change and recognize that frequently opportunities are cleverly disguised in change. All that is required to find the opportunities is openness and effort. View change as a challenge to help you learn and grow.

- Monitor your attitude with vigilance. Not doing so is similar to trying to drive a car that has no gas—you will not get to your desired destination.

- It has been said that your attitude dictates your altitude. Develop an assertive attitude and soar like an eagle.

Assertive Self-presentation

Careful attention to this dimension of assertiveness cannot be over-emphasized. Self-presentation has to do with your general physical appearance. It encompasses dress, grooming, hygiene, poise, posture, movement and demeanor. Think back, do you remember how you presented yourself when you went for that interview for a job you had to get?

Sure, you took great pride in preparing yourself, intellectually, emotionally and physically. You "dressed to impress." Why? Because you knew that it was possibly your only chance to make a great impression. You knew that the manner in which you presented yourself would dictate how the interviewer would respond to you. Your success to a large extent results from how others respond to you. Some basic principles to adhere to are:

- Set and maintain a personal standard for self-presentation.

- Always think about the impression and message that you want to convey about who you are in any environment.

- Be sure that your hair, nails, etc. are neatly groomed.

- Pay attention to overall personal hygiene including oral hygiene.

- Wear clean, unwrinkled, well-fitting clothing that is appropriate for the occasion.

- Wear shoes that are clean, comfortable and complement your clothing.

- Adopt an assertive posture when sitting. Do not slouch and always monitor your knees. Avoid crossing your legs and folding your arms as you may be viewed as not being open and receptive.

- Keep your head up, pay attention, look alert and interested.

- Project confidence, and show respect.

- Enter and leave a room with confidence. Walk with a purpose in your stride—briskly, with even strides, shoulders back, head up and a pleasant facial expression.

- Shake hands firmly but not painfully.

- Politely and respectfully initiate conversation and speak in a pleasant, clear, confident voice.

• Let your self-presentation convey the message, "I am a confident, purposeful, sensitive and approachable professional."

Remember you are your own best marketing agent, so master the art of effective self–presentation. You know yourself better than anyone else does.

Knowledge

This dimension of assertiveness reflects your intellect and business savvy. Your ability to succeed depends upon your scope or depth of knowledge and your effectiveness in applying this knowledge with efficiency, integrity and sensitivity. Assertiveness in this dimension can quickly catapult you to the top of the success ladder. The key principles for visible assertiveness in this dimension are:

• Know your business inside and out, and communicate your knowledge intelligently, sensitively and coherently.

• Establish standards of excellence and use them to guide the application of your knowledge and your operating style. Let integrity and credibility be core features in all your encounters and operations. Be true to your word and your process.

• Articulate your accomplishments with finesse. Do not exaggerate.

• Sensitively showcase your talents and skills by making creative suggestions or volunteering to do an innovative project.

• When in a business setting, keep discussions businesslike not personal. Never criticize others.

• Stay abreast with current trends and advances and share your knowledge openly but not boastfully.

- Learn and use the buzzwords and lingo of the business environment as appropriate and consistent with standards.

- Always engage in critical thinking to be objective.

- Educate yourself in good business etiquette and practice it.

- Know your purpose and remain focused. Let your attributes speak for you.

- Network and share with others. This reflects confidence and a sense of security. The more you share, the more you learn, grow and increase your visibility.

As you have seen, assertiveness has different dimensions. However, it is of paramount importance that all the dimensions be congruent in order for you to present that attractive and effective image of the assertive professional woman. I challenge you to explore, discover and redefine yourself as the brilliant gem that you are. Affirm yourself and enjoy the new assertive professional woman that you have become. Remember! Your success is in your own hands.

Personal Power Formula

Use this "personal power formula" to keep you focused—MSRF= MCES. These letters stand for: My Success Results From My Contribution in Every Situation

EXAMPLES OF ASSERTIVENESS AND NON-ASSERTIVENESS		
DIMENSION	**ASSERTIVE**	**NON-ASSERTIVE**
Verbal Communication		
Saying "No"	Refuse in clear, respectful, pleasant manner	Agree to something you do not want, feel guilty, over-apologetic
Stating Opinion	State opinion boldly, with confidence. Respectfully allow others to state theirs	Hesitant to express opinion, invests in getting approval for own opinion, easily swayed from own opinion
Advocating	Strong advocate for self. Clear, precise, tenacious	Unclear, give in easily, seek validation
Attitude	Take control Accept responsibility, prioritize, make decisions	Decisions based upon others' priorities and opinions
Feedback	Accept feedback confidently, learn from it, challenge respectfully	Absorb all feedback valid or not, grumble but never - challenge, use it to support low self-esteem
Self-presentation		
Posture	Walk purposefully, shoulders back, head up, attentive, good eye contact, exude confidence	Lethargic walk, shoulders slouched, little or no eye contact, inattentive
Attire	Neat, well groomed, appropriately dressed	Sloppily dressed, attire uncoordinated, hair, nails etc. not well groomed
Knowledge Business Savvy	Operate with integrity, high standards, objective, secure, flexible	Operate inconsistently, no set standards, subjective, rigid, insecure
Marketing	Showcase knowledge, skills and accomplishments coherently, network, participate, share, take risks	Downplay accomplishments; tentative, non-specific, hesi-tant to share, network and participate in unfamiliar activities, does not take risk

Exercise

Write a brief statement about any insights you have gained about your level of assertiveness:

_____

_____

_____

Identify any improvements that you need to make to become more assertive:

_____

_____

_____

Make a contract with yourself to work to achieve the improvements within a specific and realistic timeframe.

_____

_____

_____

_____

_____

_____

_____

_____

_____

_____

ABOUT THE AUTHOR

DR. MAMIE SHIELDS NORMAN

Dr. Shields Norman is the library media specialist and technology coordinator at Thomas Johnson Middle School in Lanham, Maryland, Prince George's County Public Schools. She serves as adjunct faculty at Sojourner-Douglass College in Annapolis, Maryland and is the owner/CEO of The Shields Group, LLC, an educational and personal development consulting firm.

Dr. Shields Norman owns and operates a pre-K Montessori weekend school. She has presented various workshops on early childhood and independence in the very young child.

Certification in the following areas qualifies Dr. Shields Norman to be of great service to many: Leadership Skills for Women, Becoming the Assertive Woman, Self-esteem and Self-empowerment, pre-K Montessori, and Anger Management for Young People. She serves on the Board of the Professional Woman Network.

Dr. Shields Norman is a native of Memphis, Tennessee and the sixth child of seven. She currently resides in Bowie, Maryland with her two sons Yohance and Zikomo. Dr. Shields Norman holds a Bachelor's degree in Sociology from Tuskegee University, a Master's in Library Science from Atlanta University, a Master's in Elementary Education American International College; Master's in Guidance and Psychological Services from Springfield College, and is AMI-certified as pre-K Montessori. She is currently awaiting the conferment of doctorate of education from NOVA Southeastern University.

Contact:
The Shields Group, LLC
3540 Crain Hwy.
Bowie, Maryland 20716
msnorman4@earthlink.net

NINE

CREATING AND COMMUNICATING YOUR VISION

By Dr. Mamie Shields Norman

Have you been carrying a dream, goal, desire or vision in your heart? How long have you had this vision in your heart and mind? Do you want to give birth to this dream/vision in a way that will bring you joy, happiness, a sense of fulfillment, and purpose in life?

It is very possible that you have been afraid to step out and reach for the essence of your vision to create and communicate so that it can become real in your life. Today, your time has come and the information which I share with you will help you see why and how you can create and communicate your vision so "those who read it can run."

And the Lord answered me and said, "Write the vision, and make it plain upon the tablets, that he may run that reads it. For the vision is yet for an appointed time, but at the end is, shall speak, and not lie. Though it tarry, wait for it; because it will surely come, it will not tarry." Habakkuk 2:2-3 (Hayford, 1995). It is certain that most people have heard it said: "Where there is no vision, the people perish."

Did you know that your vision is already inside of you? All you have to do is to discover your vision and share it with others. Most people have ideas and visions of accomplishing much and reaching personal goals. (Goals are visions which have become clear and have been written down). Once your vision becomes your written goal then there is a plan of action to follow and guide you. It could be opening your own business, completing school (or starting college for the first time) or pursuing that which has become clear and has been written down. Whatever the vision is, *write it down*. When you write down your vision, it becomes your goal and is crystallized. You are able to see it clearly.

Seeing your vision will keep you focused, encouraging you as you go through the process of developing the necessary skills and experiences you will need to perform your vision well. Also, when you write your vision, members of your family can see it and run with it. That is, they will help you achieve your vision and become a part of your vision. Everyone will be of one accord. Since you were born (and even before the foundations of the earth), your vision has been inside of you. Today, your vision is going to become alive.

What is a vision? According to Bennis, Warren and Goldsmith in their book, *Learning to Lead*, "a vision is a picture that can be seen with the mind's eye." Most of what we take into our minds is through our eyes. Our eyes are the windows of our souls and minds. The power of the eye and its use will draw others to our dreams or visions. What do you envision for your life and the impact on those around you? Is this vision clear in your mind and are others drawn to your vision?

Creating and Communicating Your Vision

How does one make her vision come alive? How does one create and communicate her vision? Following are a few simple steps to be taken which will guide anyone seeking to fulfill her dream, goal or vision in life. If the following steps are taken, then you will be on the road to creating and communicating your vision for your life:

STEP I: Determine what it takes to discover your vision

What does it take to create a vision? In creating a vision consider the following criteria adapted from Bennis, Warren and Goldsmith:

• Your vision captures your heart and your spirit. All of the issues of life flow through your heart which is spoken through the spirit. So look carefully and closely to what is in your heart and who is guiding your heart. (Realize that what is in the heart will flow from the mouth.) It will be communicated verbally when it is clear in your mind.

• Your vision speaks to what you have inside of you. The true power in creating and communicating your deepest concerns, desires and needs (which could be the very same concerns, desires and needs of someone else), is when they become alive in you as well as in someone else who shares the same vision. Each of you would have a part to play in addressing the desires, concerns and needs of others whom you are called to serve.

Creating and Communicating Your Vision

• Your vision speaks your desires. Whatever is inside of you, placed there by the Creator, (that is clearly your desire to create) will be spoken by you and no one else.

• Your vision is clearly your purpose in life as you journey on planet earth.

• You are only here for a short while. You must clearly see and walk in your purpose. Without a vision to provide meaning to the work you do or the service you render, then your work or service is senseless, meaningless, boring, and you are undoubtedly quite unhappy.

• Your vision is not complicated. It is plain to you and to those who will read and run with it. (Those who will help you along the way.)

• Your vision is fluid, dynamic and expansive. If your vision does not make you feel excited about it or life (and you do not have a passion for it), then it is not your vision. A vision is something you are passionate about, you feel it with your total being and you are excited about it when you speak it to your family and friends. You think of many ways your vision can grow, expand and reach out.

• Your vision is not clear in the beginning, but it becomes clearer and more specific as it becomes clear in your heart, mind and soul.

Creating and Communicating Your Vision

• Your vision will be birthed once you begin to see the detailed plans, goals and activities that will be implemented.

• Your vision will be a quality beyond expectation because of your passion and this passion will only demand the very best of what you are and what you have to give. There will a dedication so strong that your vision will always, next to God, remain your top priority. Your passion and dedication will be so great that nothing will get you off track. You will stay focused until the vision becomes a reality.

STEP II: Self-examination

Your vision will be uniquely your own. In creating it, take a risk, be daring and reach for what you truly want for your life (as you seek that which has already been placed in your life). Your vision will speak to your need and the needs of others, and to the strivings and hopes that are held within. To help you see that your vision is uniquely your own, and to give it power, take the time to answer the following questions:

A. What is so very different about you that makes you unique?

_____

_____

_____

B. Can you identify all of the hidden talents that are inside of you?

_____

_____

_____

C. Can you identify the needs of the people you plan to serve?

_____

_____

_____

D. What abilities, skills, experiences and talents do you have that can meet the needs of the people you plan to serve?

_____

_____

_____

E. What do you really want in your life? (i.e. joy, peace of mind, financial freedom, wisdom, spiritual or material prosperity)

_____

_____

_____

F. What are you speaking into your life?

_____

_____

_____

G. In your entire lifetime, what do you really want to achieve?

_____

_____

_____

H. The element of time is one factor standing between your vision and the realization of your vision. Look at time another way. Time is the distance between the past and NOW and it is also the distance between the future and NOW. The time of the past has shaped your vision and the time of the future will communicate your vision. So what do you plan to do during the between time, WHICH IS NOW, that will create and communicate your vision?

_____

_____

_____

I. Can you list all of the experiences (good and bad) that have influenced your vision? Keep in mind that all you have done and accomplished up to this point in your life has been the laying of the foundation of your vision. (I encourage you not to abandon all of your life's experiences. They are designed to teach you lessons in life, and to help you to create and communicate your vision.)

_____

_____

_____

J. How many steps have you taken that will lead to the creation and communication of your vision?

_____

_____

_____

K. How is your thinking? Do you think BIG or do you think small? If you think small about the vision that God has placed in your heart, then you are putting limits on God and what He can do in your life (and how He can make your vision become a reality). List some of your thoughts that have put a limit on what God can do in your life. Be honest with yourself. You can't fool God. He knows your heart.

_____

_____

_____

L. Throughout our lives, many obstacles and serious challenges confront us. They are set before us to help us grow stronger, and to grow spiritually. With our spiritual growth we are able to see clearly the vision(s) God places in our hearts and minds. Can you list some obstacles and challenges which have enhanced your spiritual growth?

_____

_____

_____

STEP III: Write your vision

Listen to the words of the prophet Habakkuk. "Write the vision, and make it plain upon the tablets that he may run that reads it; because it will surely come, it will not tarry." (Hayford,1995) God has planted in each of our hearts ideas (visions) and direction to reach out to others with the vision so that they can help us actualize it. In writing out your vision, in essence you are structuring a business plan and a portfolio, which will be presented to the population you want to serve. (Perhaps your vision may be presented to public school officials, principals, guidance counselors, business communities, social agencies, or political organizations.) Make a list of the prospective population(s) you plan to serve. Next, make an appointment to present your vision to these organizations and encourage them to understand that your vision is a perfect match for an organization seeking improvement in student behavior, academic performance, or staff interpersonal relations. (Or perhaps your vision includes the homeless, child abuse, stray animals, or tutoring newly arrived immigrants.)

_____

_____

_____

_____

_____

STEP IV: Share the vision

Share your vision with your family, friends, co-workers, and others who will receive, run with it and help you achieve your goal. When these individuals can see your vision, then each of you will be able to pull in the same direction. Make a list of those with whom you plan to share your vision.

_____

_____

_____

_____

_____

_____

REMEMBER:
• **Your vision must be written.** (Plan of action)
• **Your vision must be clear.** (Understandable)
• **Your vision must be motivating.** (Inspiring)
• **Your vision must be received with patience.** (Key to success)
• **Your vision must reflect your purpose.** (Desired goal)

You are a visionary born with a purpose and a vision! Create (discover) it and comunicate it now! See yourself moving from the idealistic to the realistic, which will bring about a big change in your life! It is up to you to mobilize your vision, so, get going and go with God, who placed the vision in your heart!

Resources
Bennis, Warren and Goldsmith, Joan. (1997) *Learning to Lead. Cambridge, Massachusetts.*

Calvaly Netbreak (2004). *Getting a Vision.* Retrieved from http://www.calvarynetbrea.org/o11101.html.

Hayford, Jack W., ed. (1995) *Spirit-filled Life Bible.* King James Version. Nashville: Thomas Nelson Publishers.

Tolle, Eckhart. (1999) *The Power of Now.* Novato, California: New World Library.

ABOUT THE AUTHOR

ELIZABETH M. WATERBURY, P.E., P.P., C.M.E.

Elizabeth Waterbury is the President and founder of E. M. Waterbury & Associates Consulting Engineers, a successful Consulting Engineering firm specializing in Land Use and Land Use Development. The focus of her career is to provide quality professional engineering services with a commitment to innovation and personal attention. Ms. Waterbury's firm consists of a talented group of female professionals and support staff who have made their mark in this specialized field of engineering, which is highly competitive and dominated by larger engineering firms.

When not working in her firm, Ms. Waterbury mentors others in professionalism, leadership and balance. This is accomplished through her many and diverse roles that vary from university professor to providing speeches as a member of The Professional Woman International Speakers Bureau. Her unique ability to channel her technical mind into creative and down-to-earth communication allows her to mentor to a broad range of individuals. One of her most honored rolls was to be the keynote speaker for the Southwest Regional Conference for the Society of Woman Engineer's. She has also been honored as a member of the International Advisory Board for The Professional Woman Network since 1990.

Her most cherished role is that of mother. She has worked hard since her daughter's birth to raise her daughter while running her firm. She is well versed in the difficulties that face women who wish to pursue their career, as well as be active in their family's lives. Her message of balance, defining personal success, and personal empowerment is carried through in all of her endeavors.

Elizabeth Waterbury

Contact:
Elizabeth Waterbury, P.E., P.P., C.M.E.
E.M. Waterbury & Associates, P.A.
17 Monmouth Street
Red Bank, NJ 07701
(732) 747-6530
fax: (732) 747-6778
EMWAssoc@aol.com
www.protrain.net

TEN

STARTING A BUSINESS

By Elizabeth M. Waterbury

The idea of starting a business for yourself is exciting and empowering. The concepts of controling your employment, executing your idea, practicing your profession with only personal restrictions, or developing and promoting your own product are only some of the reasons that entice people to entertain the exciting chapter of starting their own business. Whatever your reason, my goal in this chapter is to guide you through the rewards, challenges, steps and common pitfalls for getting started.

As a Civil Engineer specializing in Land Use and Land Development, I work on a daily basis to bring my clients from dream to reality. In order to do this I am usually a member of a team of professionals who guide our clients from the blank page, to idea, to physical reality. Although each project is unique in the nature of the development, and the community to which it resides, the general steps for each project are similar and can be placed in the following categories:

- Determine the nature of the project
- Determine the location of project
- Review feasibility
- Develop a concept plan
- Prepare the detailed plan
- Obtain required approvals
- Execute the plan

I would call these steps the "who, what, when, where, why and how" of a project, with the added step of—"get it done."

In the following sections I am going to review with you the mechanics of starting a business. But before I do that, I want to share with you some of the intangible aspects of the process. Chances are that your new business will start as a small business and remember that the founder will need to wear many hats.

Very importantly, it does not have to be a lonely spot at the top of the business. It is easier to review and reflect on the soundness of your decisions if you have a sounding board to listen and advise. Surround yourself with support. In my instance, I have a relative who had started several businesses on his own that guided me through some rocky terrain while I created the business. I also met regularly with other heads of small companies in my profession to share successes and discuss how different situations are handled. I often get new ideas and information that could be hard to get otherwise. There are also several public agencies that are in existence that are very helpful. The federal government sponsors the Small Business Administration (SBA) which is a wonderful resource. Their website is located at www.sba.gov. They have articles, course offerings, links to regulatory agencies, and a FAQ section that is very informative. Should you desire a more personal touch, there is a group of retired volunteers that guide you and share their experiences. There are identified by the initials SCORE (Service Corps of Retired Executives). SCORE is a group that is comprised of retired executives that volunteer their time to assist small business owners. Their main base is in Washington DC. Their website is www.score.org. Again, their site is very informative, but the website also lists the locations of the chapter groups that may be located within your area. There you can go and receive face-to-face assistance with your business setup and operation. There is a lot to know when running a business. You don't have to go it alone.

As a woman, you will find that some of the traditional formats of running a business may not be appropriate for you. In my instance, it is not uncommon for clients to be treated to a game of golf, then retreat to the "19th hole" for a cocktail. Most of my clients are men. I am fairly athletic so playing golf was not an issue. The issue came when they retreated for the cocktail. First, the 19th hole was through the men's locker room, and second, many of the spouses of the men did not appreciate me hanging in the bar with their guys. I had to find another way. In this instance the traditional form of entertaining did not suit my personal business.

You may find similar or other types of situations that require a different touch. Surrounding yourself with the support of other women in business can help guide you through this. The Small Business Administration offers support information for women-run businesses at their website www.onlinewbc.gov. As a part of this website there is a listing of various associations that relate to women in businesses. This can be found at www.onlinewbc.gov/womens_business.html. Again, you can look and see which one has a chapter in your area.

Is it for you?

When starting a business it is important to take that hard look at yourself and your goals to decide if your personality and situation are ones that can support the effort that is needed. Here are some questions to ask yourself:

1. **What is the nature of your personality?** Are you independent and able to be confident in your decisions? Are you outgoing and able to handle risk without undo stress? Are you a self-motivated person? Starting and maintaining your own business requires that you accept that no one is going to do it for you. You are responsible for taking the actions.

2. **How do you handle conflict?** If you shy away from conflict, then running a business may not be right for you. Small business owners need to handle issues that arise whether they be with a client, employee or vendor.

3. **Can your lifestyle and commitments fare with a reduction in income?** It can take months and maybe years to develop steady based income. You should assess if this could negatively impact your lifestyle or commitments. Remember the U.S. Small Business Administration notes that 50% of all businesses fail in the first year, and 95% fail within 5 years.

4. **What is the state of your physical and emotional condition?** Are you able to handle the stress and the long hours that usually come hand-in-hand with having your own business? As I noted in the beginning, starting a business is exciting and empowering. However, it is a lot of work. You will require stamina to work the hours needed for the startup. Sometimes the long hours and seemingly slow results can cause you to feel down. You need to be a person with a positive personality to weather those moments and get moving again.

5. **Have you reviewed the effects of starting a business with family members or other significant relations that would be impacted by your decision?** Many times the long hours and stress of the business can cause strain on the owner's family and/or their significant relationships. Especially in the beginning, you are always at work. If you are not at it, you are thinking about it. As noted above, starting a business and being a business owner can be very stressful. Should your life outside of work not support the effort needed to perform the required tasks, then this will make the journey even more difficult.

6. **Are you good at multi-tasking?** A business owner generally juggles several tasks at once. This requires organization and planning.

7. **Are you willing to look at yourself and assess your strengths and weaknesses?** The courage to look within yourself and validate your strengths and work on your weaknesses is vital to the strength of your company. It will only be as strong as your weakest trait.

8. **Are you willing to learn and change?** Owning a business is a journey. It is always in movement. Each day will bring something new. A new challenge to overcome. You can learn from all around you. Even when you think you have arrived, your journey continues in order to maintain it. You will need to change as the times change around you. As you have probably noticed, the questions above are about you—who you are, what you are like. (They are not about your skills, or expertise for your field of training.) They are hard questions to consider, but they are important ones.

So after you have answered the questions above, there are two more to ask yourself: *How do I define my personal success and happiness? Does starting a business fit into my picture of success and happiness?*

I believe the ultimate goal in a person's life is to be happy and live a life that meets their concept of success. This means different things to different people. Some may find happiness and a successful life in the relationships they experience whether they are at work or at home. Others may find their sense of success through their artistic achievements; others through their financial achievements. As you look to make a new chapter for yourself, recognize that the choices you make for your business affect you as an individual. Always keep a sense of your underlying goal as you define your business. You will be more successful, in a global sense, with the business being a part of your happiness rather than waiting to step away from the business to enjoy life.

Developing your Business Plan

Now that I said my piece about those types of items, I would like to get down to the mechanics of starting the business. A business plan is essential for starting a business. Through the preparation of a business plan you will be able to define the "who, what, where, when and whys" for your businesses. The business plan will be the blueprint for the implementation of your business. Besides organizing your thoughts and defining your tasks for starting the business, many financial institutions will require this document to assess the risk associated with your proposal. The plan is also valuable in proposing your business to possible partners, and obtaining business sites.

In order to begin you must first understand your purpose for going into business. As noted in the first paragraph, there are several types of reasons that people strike out on their own. These can include:

• Personal control of your employment

• Freedom of personal expression

• Practicing your profession with only personal restrictions

• Developing and promoting your own product

The goals of the company should be in concert with the original purpose for starting the business. The creation of a mission statement will define for yourself and others the nature and purpose of your business. The mission statement is a brief, concise description of the essence of your business. This will determine the "why" of the company. It is hard to clearly move on to the "what" you are going to do, if you haven't defined the "why."

Once you have decided *why* you want to start a business, the next logical step is to determine *what* it is you are to do. I have spent quite a bit of time discussing the aspects of individual knowledge. It is important that you also have a thorough understanding of the product or service that you are to provide. This is easier if you are looking to spin- off a business within the trade you are presently practicing. This is more difficult if you are looking to start anew outside the trade topic. In this instance I would look to yourself to see what you are particularly good at doing, a hobby you would like to expand, or a particular niche that is correct for you. I have heard many an engineering joke about the stereotype of the analytical mind. As much as I like to think I do not fully fall within that category, I find that the basis for those jokes is innate within me, or I could not do the job.

As a municipal engineer, I must be a "people person" as well as an analytical one. We are a rare breed. I joke that I was a cross of an engineer (my father) and a politician (my mother) and, therefore, I was bred for the job. Although some may feel that I became an engineer and then became analytical, I feel that each type of personality is geared for the particular job or profession. Therefore, I became a municipal engineer because I am analytical, creative and love people, and this profession gave me an outlet for all of these personality traits. The true test is that when I have had to spend long periods of time at home, I drive my husband nuts by having to create and recreate our home. I have to have an outlet. My purpose here is to outline that there is a trade or profession that is innate in you. It is something that you love and that is natural for you. This is a good choice for your business.

Another key decision is whether you are going to go it alone or with a partner. This is somewhat separate from the discussion of the type of business you may have that will follow shortly. The decision to have a partner is important as the joining into a business relationship is a marriage of sorts and should not be taken lightly. I suggest that any partner that you choose be of a personality type where you can complement each other, respect and trust each other's skills, have common purpose and goals for the company, and be able to work out conflict in a reasonable manner. I come from an entrepreneurial family and have observed many a business go bad because of the wrong choice of partners. Any partnership should have a partnership agreement associated with it. This should define the ownership, dissolving of partnership procedure, and fate of the partnership should one partner die. Have your own attorney review the partnership agreement for you to be sure that your rights have been properly protected.

Although some may not wish to discuss the issues associated with the break up of a partnership, it is best to outline these issues in the beginning so that the outline is set when you are all feeling good about the partnership. If you are choosing a significant other, spouse or close friend to be your partner, be sure you do not ignore this step of the partnership agreement. This is a business and your livelihood. The break up of a friendship or marriage without the agreement can complicate an already emotional situation. As noted before, 95% of all businesses fail within the first five years. Although detailed planning and research at the startup of the business improves your odds of being in the successful 5%, the odds are against the business and it is best to plan for the possibility.

Types of Business

There are three types of businesses. Each has it own advantages and disadvantages. You should research each to see which is appropriate for you.

1) **Sole Proprietorship under your own name.** With this form of business you are practicing under your own name. The start up is inexpensive and there are fewer regulations governing the business. However, you do not have protection from personal liability. This form of business is generally not required to be registered for a business name with the state. However, there are filing requirements with the Departments of Labor. Check with your state to see what time frames are required.

2) **Sole Proprietorship or General Partnership using a trade name.** With this form the business name is generally different than the individual(s) or may include the designation of "Company." The founder(s) choose(s) a trade name and operate(s) trading as that named entity. The name is filed with the County Clerk's office. Again, these are easy to formulate and have low start up costs. Again, there is no protection from personal liability as you are the company.

3) **Corporation, Limited Liability Company, and Limited Liability Partnership.** There are two forms of corporations, one is an 'S' corporation the other is a 'C' corporation. There are advantages and disadvantages to each, primarily tax related. These forms of company afford the owners limited liability exposure. These forms are closely regulated by the government and can be expensive to set up. The 'S'

corporation is a simpler form of a corporation. These forms are required to maintain extensive records and have regular filing requirements with the Department of Labor and the IRS.

Now that you have the basics addressed, you can prepare your business plan. The following is an outline of the basics to include. Please note the Business Plan is the document that sells your business. Take time in preparing it. Be thorough in your descriptions of the sections so that the reader can walk away with a detailed understanding of your business and how you propose to execute the start up and operation.

I. Introduction –The introduction should be a summary of the type of business, product or services offered, mission statement, start up date, the owners information, business location, and general description of the business and goals.

II. Company Description –The company description should include a detailed description of the business and the product or services offered. This would include the organization of the business and the responsibilities and expertise of the key members. A description of the detailed operation of the business should be provided. Also, you should include in this section any uniqueness that sets your product or service apart from others in your field.

III. Marketing Analysis–This relates to the feasibility of success for your product or service in the location proposed. The analysis should address the availability of similar services in the area and compare it to the area's needs. If you have hired others to perform an assessment of this type, then this should be affixed to the report for review.

IV. Marketing Strategies–Describe your plan for marketing your business and bringing in clients.

V. Financial Requirements and Management–This section should discuss the budgeted costs associated with the start up and the anticipated funds needed to get the business operational and independent. I noted earlier that it can be months and maybe years before the business can thrive on its own. Take this into account when assessing your needs. Your vision for the operation of the business should match the ability to acquire funding and repay any loans to support that operation. It is a delicate balance that has broken many a business. Please note, financial institutions may require the personal financial information relating to the individual(s) starting the business. Since it is a new business without a track record, they may require personal guarantees to cover their exposure. Review those guarantees with all impacted parties prior to committing to them.

VI. Conclusions–Provide your conclusions on the business plan. This may include projections of where the business is to be over certain periods of time. Projections will provide you with goals to reach for. A caution however: When a business is new, it can be difficult to define its future so be conservative with any projections you offer to make them as realistic as possible. The success or failure of a business is controlled by so many factors, many of which are not within your control. A rule of thumb is that it generally will take longer and cost more than you think from the beginning. Allow yourself room. Don't start off by making unrealistic expectations that could never be met that are based upon what you want to happen, not what can happen.

Now that you have assessed all the details and formulated your plan, it is time to go do it. Your business will have as much positive energy as you put into it. No one is more interested in what happens with it than you, so let everyone know that. I am happy to say that this past January, I celebrated the ten-year anniversary of my engineering firm. The time flew. I would note that my firm is comprised mainly of men and women who are the primary caregivers for their families and who want to continue their professions. Many telecommute from home. Many work odd hours to coincide with their desires to be available for their children. This is unheard of in the engineering world. Many thought I was nuts when the company was founded and molded into the type of company it is today. Time has shown that I am not nuts.

Our firm is unique. We do what we do because we love it. And we do it our way. You can, too.

Notes:

ABOUT THE AUTHOR

MARTHA BARRETT

Martha (Marti) Barrett is Vice President of Market Development for Bank of America in Jacksonville, Florida. She is also an elected member of the Duval County School Board.

She is a graduate of Maryville University with a Bachelors degree in Political Science and received her Masters degree in Education from Xavier University in Cincinnati, Ohio.

Ms. Barrett is also a Public Image Consultant, certified through The Professional Woman Network in Louisville, KY. She has also studied under Dorothea Johnson, President of the Protocol School of Washington.

She has presented topics such as corporate image, etiquette, table manners and networking tips to many local groups including Youth Leadership Jacksonville, First Coast Manufacturers, Junior League, Jacksonville University, University of North Florida, Florida Engineers Society and Florida Community College.

She is a recipient of the "World of Girl Scouting Award" from Gateway Girl Scouts Council, YWCA Award—Tribute to Women, 25 Most Influential Women in 2004 from the Jacksonville Business Journal, Community Service Award from the First Coast Manufacturers and the Leadership Award from Leadership Jacksonville.

Ms. Barrett serves on several non-profit boards, including Museum of Science and History, Cultural Council of Greater Jacksonville, Ritz Theatre Board, Florida House Board and Leadership Florida Board.

Contact:
5201 Atlantic Blvd. #277
Jacksonville, FL 32207
(904) 343-7846
barrettm@educationalcentral.org

ELEVEN

NETWORKING & VISIBILITY

By Martha E. Barrett

When you are networking or at a business function, people look at you and form an impression. When they hear your voice, they think of an image. Image is not just about how you look and speak, but how you behave as well. Observing business etiquette at any networking function is an important part of a professional image. But often people haven't learned proper etiquette. (If you know business etiquette, you have such an advantage over your competitors.) Some people think that etiquette is just for bluebloods or the wealthy, but it is for everyone.

Networking tips:
• Make sure you give a firm handshake and wear your nametag on the right shoulder.

• If your employer sends you to a social and "business" function, go and network. You have wasted your employer's time if you have not promoted your company.

• In networking, kindness and courtesy count.

• One needs to understand that to network, one needs to be a good listener. You need to be able to make "small talk." A conversation about everyday occurrences!

• Women get stuck at these networking occasions over the "kiss." Consider this: You are a woman at a business function and you see a distinguished businessman. He greets you with a handshake and kiss on the cheek and a friendly hello. Proper or not? This is a real characteristic of the South. It's certainly not a put down. Instead, it is a sign of respect. But if "The Kiss" (and it is on on the cheek) falls outside of your comfort zone, it can be received with a sincere smile and a firm friendly extension of a hand for shaking.

• When a young woman enters the business world, how does she gain visibility within the company? Doing a good job representing the company at any networking or business function is a strong manner in which to gain visibility needed for upward mobility.

• Join professional organizations that match your interests and needs.

• The Chamber of Commerce is a great networking organization. Their "Business After Hours" socials or their luncheons are a great source for new friends and business contacts.

• The National Association for Female Executives is a very well-respected national group and provides strong venues for networking on a local and regional basis. A most interesting and informative magazine "The Executive Female" is sent to all members.

- The Junior League is another excellent group. Not only is it socially-based, but their real mission is to raise money for various charities. As an altruistic organization, you will meet other like-minded young women who wish to raise money for good causes.

- You will gain community visibility and warm your own heart by volunteering for the American Heart Association or American Cancer Society. Such types of "disease" groups are very active and people are passionate about them.

I became active in the American Cancer Society as Chairman of the annual "Jail and Bail" fundraiser. This fundraiser "jailed" people and the arrested folks called from their "jail" cell for bail. Though this was a huge undertaking, I met so many friends that way. (This was back in 1988 and I still have acquaintances whom I met through that event.) You find that people who are interested in non-profits are good people. They want to help others. Those are the kind of friends you want! If you successfully chair a fundraiser you are immediately noticed. I was asked to be on the board of the American Cancer Society as a result of Jail and Bail! You have to start out somewhere. If you are successful on one board, often other boards want you!

- Every organization—even non-profits—have politics involved. People aren't perfect. But just stick to your guns, have patience, know your goals, and understand that politics are usually part of the "game."

- Always work hard and tell the truth. Be positive about events and enjoy the moment!

- When a woman has joined boards and is well known, she just might be ready to run for political office!

That's what I did in 2000. I ran for the Duval County School Board, even though I had been involved in politics for many years, and never thought I would run for political office! But never say never! I met with the man who wanted to run for the same political office, and I told him, "Let the best person win!" I worked hard and he didn't seem to work as hard (from my viewpoint). I qualified to run for the office in July 2000 and he ended up not qualifying, so I automatically won! This was a great testament to me about how all the hard work I had done in the community paid off!

People gave me contributions and even went door-to-door for me in June and July in Florida! (This takes real commitment as it is so unbearably hot!) It showed me that when you dedicate yourself to doing well in a community, then the community rewards you! I won unopposed in 2004 as well and became Chairman of the Duval County School Board in 2003–2004. All of these are great experiences and certainly taught the importance of hard work.

Tips on Networking a Room

- When you go to a business reception remember that it is business first and not a social occasion. Although you do socialize, this reception is meant for you to branch out and network with people you do not know.

- When you arrive at the reception do not go to the first person you know and stick with him or her all night! Go up to people you don't know—introduce yourself and be engaging!

- Initially engage in a light conversation. (I call this "chit chat.") Then find out the interests of the person and really enjoy communicating with him/her! You can exchange cards and realize you may have just met a good contact!

- You never know who you will meet! (Be prepared to meet people from different business levels, backgrounds, and cultures.)

- In this day and age, people do not stay in one job for very long. You may be surprised by someone who was impressed with you at a networking/business function, calling you and offering you a job.

- Do not drink a lot of alcohol. These are business events and you don't want to embarrass yourself or your company!

- Make sure you write a thank you note to the host! This will really set you a part from the crowd! No e-mail or voice mail—a handwritten note!!

Join a Political Campaign

I have never met more people than when I've been involved with a political campaign. A campaign has a finite ending. Everyone knows when the election will take place. (There is such an emotional feeling on election night when your candidate wins!!)

In a campaign, everyone works for the same candidate. Some go door to door, some fundraise, and some call people on the phone. You get to know people so well and you make great friends and contacts. Sometimes you will even get a job from the campaign!

Get to be an Expert on an Issue

If you are a CPA, a broker or lawyer or any professional person, you should get to know some media people and let them know your expertise so that they will call you when they are doing an article or television segment about that field. Your name gets into the newspaper and before you know it, people will recognize your name and will call upon you when they are needing a person with your skills and knowledge.

Keep in mind the importance of networking, community involvement and representing your company in business/social settings. You will gain more power and visibility if you continue to be aware of the importance of keeping your image and self out in front of others. Take the first step to being involved! Good luck!

Notes:

ABOUT THE AUTHOR

NYDA BITTMANN-NEVILLE

Nyda Bittmann-Neville is president and founder of TNB Consulting Group, Inc. a global organization specializing in innovative marketing, communications, and image solutions.

The firm, established in 1996, has created, designed and implemented customized marketing strategies for clients within the U. S., Canada and Australia. These programs have established cultures and protocol within organizations that have resulted in their communicating effectively, marketing persuasively, and projecting themselves professionally. The customized development programs have facilitated learning with more than 5,000 professionals and topics range from team building, diversity, effective communications, presentation skills, professional image, and harassment to sales and sales management. Additionally, Nyda has served in the capacity of integration manager to coordinate seven firms into one national organization; has managed business process improvement projects; and created new corporate images. Nyda is an executive coach and professional speaker.

Her innovative solutions have been implemented in the industries of financial, insurance, travel, high-tech, law, education, manufacturing, and government. A sampling of her clients include Lockheed Martin, Macquarie Investments (Australia) Delta ComAir, Greater Orlando Aviation Authority, Georgia Pacific, Barnett-Nations-Bank of America, TAL Private (Canada), Osceola County Government and School District, University of Central Florida, SunTrust and Russell Corporation.

Contact:
TNB Consulting Group, Inc.
3561 Bellington Drive
Orlando, FL 32835
(407) 298-8700
www.tnbgroup.com
www.protrain.net

TWELVE

MARKETING YOUR PERSONAL BRAND

By Nyda Bittmann-Neville

Think of marketing yourself as a painter's palette. When all the colors come together, an image appears—your image and brand. Image and brand are built by consistency. Go ahead, take a look in the mirror, stand up and see the physical image you project. Is it the image you desire? Is there room for enhancement? Regardless of the answer, please read on because you are about to gain invaluable tips and techniques to help you achieve the image and brand you desire, now and in the future!

Let's explore the colors of our palette; each one represents a different aspect of our image and brand. *Image* is how others think about you when your name is mentioned, and *brand* is the experience they have when they interact with you. Our discussion will center on the following aspects that comprise image and brand. Think of each as having a corresponding color.

- Communication = Yellow
- Presentation = Purple
- Appearance/Attitude = Blue
- Networking = Green
- Visibility = Red

Communication = yellow

Yellow is bright, cheerful, sometimes soothing, other times bold, depending on the intensity of the hue. Our communication is similar to this description and that is my reasoning behind its selection. Remember that with every way that you communicate, whether it is when you introduce yourself, tell someone about what you do for a living, answer the telephone, or respond via email or other electronic medium, your image and brand are showing.

In order to communicate effectively and create the image and brand we desire, we must first begin with how we want others to react to us. The first step is to develop our positioning statement. Now for those of you who are already thinking of putting this book to the side because it sounds like work rather than pleasure, DON'T DO IT! This exercise will be of such enormous help to you that you will be glad you survived it. In fact, you will probably wish to celebrate by having a t-shirt printed with the positioning statement on the front and back.

A positioning statement is a description of you and/or your company. It is the core message you want to deliver everywhere, including in elevators and airport waiting areas to influence others' perceptions. For many of you, becoming an entrepreneur is your goal. Therefore, I want you to realize that *you* are your company, whether your business career takes you into the corporate world, small business, or your own shop.

The positioning statement comes from the answers to seven questions.

• Who are you?

• What school or business (current or future) are you in?

• What people will you serve (current or future)?

• What are the special needs and desires of these people?

• With whom will you be or are you competing?

• What makes you different from those competitors?

• What unique benefit does an individual derive from your service (current or future) or from interacting with you?

Here is an example to jumpstart your creativity and help you through the process. Let's see how Bloomingdale's Department Store developed its positioning statement. (I use Bloomingdale's since most women enjoy shopping, and we have probably all visited one of the stores, looked at a catalogue, or visited the website.)

Bloomingdale's Positioning Statement

1. Who/what? *A fashion-focused department store*

2. Serve? *Trend-conscious, upper middle-class shoppers*

3. Their needs and desires? *Looking for high end and/or unusual, unique products*

4. Competition? *Indifference first, then other fashion-focused companies*

5. Difference? *Provide unique merchandise in a dramatic setting*

6. Unique benefit? *Turn shopping into entertainment*

Rather than make fashion the difference, Bloomingdale's chose to focus on the experience of being there. In the same way, that is your goal as you interact with individuals along your life journey.

Now create your own positioning statement. Please take the time to complete this exercise, as it is the foundation on which to build your image and brand. I have supplied you with a worksheet for convenience.

Positioning Statement

Answer these seven questions to establish your positioning statement:

• Who are you?

_____

_____

_____

• What school or business (current or future) are you in?

_____

_____

_____

• What people do you serve (current or future)?

_____

_____

_____

• What are the special needs and desires of these people?

_____

_____

_____

• With whom are you competing?

_____

_____

_____

What makes you different from those competitors?

_____

_____

_____

What unique benefit does a client derive from your service?

_____

_____

_____

This statement will serve as your continuing focus to ensure you are being consistent in your actions and behaviors, which are your image and thus your brand. After you have completed this, set the book aside, and enjoy a refreshing drink and snack. You deserve it!

Using the positioning statement, you can now branch out and develop a 30-second commercial. Your commercial will change as you progress through your life's journey. It can be created for business or personal use, or a combination of the two, depending on the situation. You will use the 30-second commercial more than you ever realized possible.

A 30-second commercial is the answer to the questions, "Tell me about yourself," "What do you do for a living?" or "I see that you work for ABC Company, and what do you do there?" The answer to any of them is your 30-second commercial. But how do you answer any of those three questions right now? Say each answer out loud, and then ask yourself, "What impact did I make on the person asking the question?" "Was my answer professional?" "Did it sound enthusiastic?" It doesn't matter how you answered the questions. Let's enhance the responses to ensure they represent the image and help build the brand you desire.

A successful and effective 30-second commercial depends on how it is delivered and the actual words used. Begin with your name, followed by what I call an *interest generating idea* (IGI). This is the creative part of the commercial. Give what you do an unexpected twist, image, or description. Because the IGI gains attention, and the listener says, "How interesting or tell me more," you need two supporting points to explain the interest you've generated. Let me give you two examples:

1. An executive assistant to the President of ABC Company introduces herself as a juggler. During the course of her day, she explains, she juggles duties such as filing, writing memos, scheduling meetings, and making telephone calls. At the end of the day, she hopes all the balls she has juggled have fallen into the right places.

2. A consumer lender in a financial institution introduces himself as a dream maker because he provides the funding that makes dreams become realities for his clients. Whether the dream is a boat, new home, or worldwide vacation, he can make it happen.

Both of these examples possess the IGI, gaining attention of the listener and making him or her want to learn more. This is the goal with your 30-second commercial. Use the Design Sheet to develop your 30-second commercial.

Design Sheet
30-Second Commercial

Introduction:

_____

_____

_____

Interest Generating Idea (IGI):

_____

_____

_____

Two Key Points:

_____

_____

_____

_____

_____

_____

Several tips:

• Always introduce yourself as "I am Susie Smith" or "I'm Susie Smith." Never introduce yourself as "My name is…," as it sounds too robotic.

• The Interest Generating Idea (IGI) should be unusual, unique, catchy, or visual, enabling the listener to see an image.

• Two key points can be sentences or phrases that support, enhance, or explain your Interest Generating Idea.

When you have created your first draft, stand up, and deliver it to the mirror. It will probably sound somewhat awkward, so say it a few times until you begin to feel comfortable. Next, try it out on someone new, and see the reaction. You will be amazed.

Now that we have completed the positioning statement and the 30-second commercial, what comes next? With your delivery of the commercial go a professional handshake and a business card. Make sure that you do not ever deliver anything but a solid handshake. No wimpy dishrags allowed! A business card is essential to look professional. If you are still in school, transitioning and/or returning to business or work, you need a business card just as someone does who is employed. Without it, how can people find you? Select a plain card on substantial paper stock and center your full name on the card with all the pertinent contact information. Never leave home without cards, and always carry them where you don't have to fumble to find one. (Fumbling through your purse or briefcase gives the impression that you are disorganized and unprepared.)

As you interact with others, your image and brand make an impression. Look at the list below and write what first comes to mind as you think of each major company or person.

Harley Davidson _____

Nike _____

Coca Cola _____

Martha Stewart _____

Oprah _____

Marlboro _____

BMW_____

Some of the comments may be positive, and others negative. In fact, some comments may be different today than what you would have written a year ago or due to different situations that have occurred. I think you can now see just how powerful image and brand really are.

Presentation = purple

Purple is a rich, royal color that commands attention. It is also magical and possesses elements of surprise. When you present your thoughts and ideas to one individual or a large group, you want to think of how you will speak. Any presentation should follow the three Cs: Clear, Concise and Compelling. Your posture should be straight, head and chin up, and you should project your voice appropriately for the size of the room and group. Make sure your sentences do not end on an upswing, but rather a strong, solid note. Practice the pitch, pace, and volume of your voice to orchestrate its effectiveness. Think of voices that you hear and just cannot listen to, and then think of other voices that you like. Model yours after those you like that maintain a strong, medium pitch and volume along with a steady pace.

Appearance and Attitude = blue

Blues represent dependability, authority, security, and calm. They are also cool and refreshing. Your appearance and attitude fall into these categories. (Although your favorite jeans provide all this each time you put them on, maybe that's not the image and brand you're looking for now or for a particular situation.)

First, you must determine your appearance style and stick to it. Remember, consistency creates a strong brand. Is your style romantic, classic, professional, casual, trendy, or traditional? What colors best compliment you? You can look in your clothes closet and select the outfits that you feel the best in, lay them out, and review the colors and styles. You will probably get a good indication of your favorite style and your best colors. If you still have trouble making these determinations there are professionals who can assist you. Ask yourself before you leave the house if your appearance matches or enhances your desired image and brand. If the answer is no, go back, and change clothes. If yes, proceed to make a positive impact on the world.

Attitude is always a key player when it comes to image and brand. Yours should be positive, not fake, but genuinely enthusiastic. Remember, you can see attitude, feel attitude, hear attitude, and almost taste attitude.

Networking = green

Green grass and trees are the foundation for nature's playground. They are stable and rich. The color green also signifies freshness and invigoration. Networking is the opportunity to introduce yourself to the world, develop relationships and assist in the success of YOU. Networking is more than just attending an event, gathering and distributing business cards, returning to the office, and adding them to the rolodex, or placing them in file 13. Networking begins with defining your objective for attending the event, having meaningful conversations, exchanging business cards when there is a reason to do so, and following up the good conversations with action.

First, determine your objective. If it is to meet three new people, then do it. Ask for a card only if you feel the connection will be beneficial. After the event, write the date/year and a brief description of the person on the card. Determine the best follow-through action: a telephone call or email; having coffee together; sending information about your product or service, or doing something you know the other person needs. For networking to continue to be fruitful, you must cultivate it similar to cultivating a healthy green garden. For years I have made Monday the day to contact at least one individual that I have not communicated with in several months. It is a great way to introduce an upbeat experience to the dreaded Monday and also reconnects you with someone.

Visibility = red

There is no time like now to increase and enhance your visibility. You have all the tools necessary to heighten the awareness of YOU! Red is a vibrant, hot color and stimulates the nervous system. This is our goal, to stimulate your actions, behaviors and activities to gain and increase visibility!

Here are several tips and techniques to accomplish this goal:

• Obtain a professional photograph for business purposes. It will be used for announcements in newspapers and magazines, speaking engagements, résumés, and so on. Never wear black or white as they are too stark. Wear a complementary color to your skin tone, hair and eye color. Take a new photograph periodically.

• Join an organization of personal or industry interest. Sign up for a committee that you feel will provide you with visibility.

• Purchase a name badge with a magnetic backing. This type reflects professionalism without putting holes or tape on your clothes. If you interchange gold and silver jewelry, purchase a matching name badge. These can be ordered with your name at most office supply stores. Always place your name badge on the right side so when you shake hands the person can view your name.

• Seek out high-profile individuals in your community, industry, school, or church and make an appointment. The purpose of the appointment is to gain insight into their success (everyone likes to share his or her story.) Develop three to five open-ended questions that you will ask every person so you can analyze the answers for trends and patterns. Some sample questions:

- What one piece of advice did you receive when you started your career that set the right course?

- What qualities and skills do you see are most important or critical in today's work environment?

- What role does one's image and brand play in the overall career of an individual?

• Create a one-page summary of each of your projects or accomplishments and place it in your personal folder. The summaries can be used to update your resume or executive profile as well as help when it comes to performance reviews. The summary should include the name of the project, date, scope and results along with your role.

• Join the corporate business club, chamber of commerce or women's organization that you feel best meets your needs. You can attend several times without joining to see if it is a good fit for you. Then get involved!

• Play a sport or develop a hobby. Whatever your choice, you can find clubs and organizations that foster the activity and offer the opportunity to network, grow, build relationships, and have fun.

• The motto for visibility is be seen, be heard, and be there!

Your palette has many different colors; some more focused and intense than others, but all are equally important to create your image and brand. The image that emerges from your painting will be strong, vibrant and yours alone!

Notes:

ABOUT THE AUTHOR

LAURA LEEZER

Laura Swanson Leezer consults professionally in the areas of clothing and figure analysis, style definition and development, non-verbal communication skills, and professional development. She has held management positions in the retail field including sales, buying, and training and is currently Vice President and Director of Marketing in the financial industry.

Ms. Leezer holds a Master's degree in education and teaches classes in fashion, marketing, and business in higher education.

Ms. Leezer is certified in diversity and women's issues by The Professional Woman Network and serves on the International Advisory Board.

Her true passion is mentoring and helping people develop their skills and talents. Her future plans include travel, writing and furthering her education which is a never-ending process.

Contact:
Laura Swanson Leezer
10680 E. 1000th Street
Macomb, IL 61455
(309) 837-2325
lauraswanson@macomb.com

THIRTEEN

WARDROBE ORGANIZATION

By Laura Swanson Leezer

The purpose of this chapter is to provide you with useful information that will allow you to establish and maintain an organized and wearable wardrobe.

You will receive helpful information that will allow you to achieve the following:

1. Define your clothing and accessory storage space.

2. Assess your clothing and accessory items.

3. Organize your current wardrobe by seasons and categories according to your life and your daily activities.

4. Develop a core clothing and accessory wardrobe.

5. Understand and define your fashion personality and develop your own personal style.

6. Utilize your existing clothes and accessories.

7. Know the difference between a trend and a classic item.

8. Select new clothing and accessories that will fit well into your current wardrobe and shop with a list.

9. Dress with enthusiasm every morning as you achieve a uniform theme from head to toe.

10. Understand useful ways to store your clothing and accessories.

The first procedure is to review and evaluate your clothing and accessories. The second portion is to examine the storage space in which you keep your items. The space in which items are stored can be a large factor in finding and utilizing your clothing and accessories to the fullest. To provoke thought regarding your clothing and accessory issues, ask yourself the following questions:

• Do you wear everything in your wardrobe at least three times a season?

• Do you have several items in your wardrobe that you have not worn in over one year?

• Do you have items in your closet that need repair such as a button, hemming, etc.

• Do you make regular trips to the dry cleaners, but when you go to your closet, realize the items are wrinkled and need pressing?

• Do you have different sizes in your current wardrobe, hoping that you will get back into your ideal size soon?

• Do you have items that still have tags on them?

• Do you have items that are out of fashion but you are keeping them in hopes they will come back into fashion?

- Do you have a closet full of clothing and accessories but still tend to wear the same items repeatedly?

- Do you have five or more of any one item? (Example: Five short black skirts)

- Do you have any items in your wardrobe that you cannot part with for sentimental reasons? (Example: Dress you wore to prom)

- Do you find that your clothes are tight and hard to move from side to side because your closet is so full?

- Do you dress in a timely manner when getting ready for your day but need more time because of clothing issues you face?

- Do you wish you had more room to store your clothing?

- Do you lose items of clothing or jewelry and later find them somewhere in your closet or hidden in the drawer?

- Do you have items in your wardrobe because:
    - a friend gave it to you
    - a friend talked you into it
    - a person you like wears one just like it
    - you saw it on TV, in the movies, or at the mall

These questions will assist you in defining your organizational needs and allow you to recognize challenge areas in your clothing and accessory wardrobe. Many times, when people go to their closets, they do not see set patterns until they are brought to their attention. If you answered yes to several of these questions, it may be time to eliminate items from your wardrobe. You may find that because of your lifestyle, you have items that you need to purchase to make your wardrobe more useful.

As we continue with the assessment portion of organizing your clothing and jewelry, keep in mind the questions you just answered "yes" to.

Clothing and Accessory Assessment

Now is the time to take an important look at the items you own. This process is not something you can rush through, so, allow yourself several hours of uninterrupted time and plenty of space. Tackle your clothing first. It is suggested that you evaluate your accessories after you finish your clothing. Accessory items include:

• Belts

• Scarves

• Purses and Briefcases

• Shoes

• Jewelry

• Undergarments

• Socks and hosiery

• Sleepwear

Each accessory category can be reviewed individually. Follow the same steps as you would with your clothing.

If you store the majority of your clothing in your bedroom, then you can utilize your bed for viewing and sorting. If you store additional clothing in another room, bring all items to your bedroom.

The viewing should take place on a large flat surface regardless of which room you use. The flat surface needs to be cleared and covered with a large white tablecloth or white sheet. Covering the surface in white allows for clear viewing of garment color. If you do not have access to such a flat surface, utilize the floor or large table covered with a white cloth. You can also utilize a sturdy rolling rack if available. The following are supplies you will need for assessment and sorting:

1. A notebook or pad of paper and pencil for writing down clothing categories and inventorying clothing according to group. You may also create a list of items that need to be added or replaced.

2. Full-length mirror

3. Laundry basket or container for items that need to be laundered

4. Bag for items that need to be taken to the cleaners

5. Bag or container for items that need to be altered or fixed

6. Garbage bag for items that need to be donated to Goodwill, The Salvation Army, a church rummage sale, or other worthy cause

7. Garbage bag for items to throw out

8. Small clear plastic bags for accessories

The supplies listed above will enable you to take an action with every item you have. Making a clear decision at this time allows for a complete inventory of what items you will have remaining at the end of the process. Make sure that you have all clothing items before you begin. Do not forget to check other storage areas, such as attics, basements, other closets, under beds, friends' or relatives' homes, cleaners, tailors, etc.

Clothing Categories

Now is the time when all garments are gathered together and separated into specific categories. Below is a list of possible categories:

1. Blouses/shirts
2. Knit tops
3. Sweaters
4. Pants
5. Jeans
6. Shorts
7. Capris/leggings
8. Skirts
9. Jackets/blazers
10. Dresses
11. Formal attire
12. Workout wear
13. Jog suits
14. Swimwear
15. Other (this area will incorporate all other clothing items)
16. Outerwear

Fashion Personality Definition

As clothing items are placed into groups, a common theme such as color, detail, silhouette, and texture, may become apparent. You may also become aware that no common theme or pattern may exist.

Common themes in your wardrobe help to define your dominant fashion personality. This will help you in your primary clothing and accessory selection. There are typically five types of fashion personalities.

They are:

- **Romantic Fashion Personality:** lace, floral prints, flowing soft fabrics, pearls, pastels, ruffles, feminine theme to dressing, ballet flats, pretty pumps in light tones, gold jewelry with filigree or detailed designs, ornate brooches, pearl necklaces and earrings, soft hair styles

- **Classic Fashion Personality:** tailored lines, simple detail, silhouettes that go season after season, jackets and matching skirts and slacks, clothes that tend to work with everything, classic pumps in black and navy, classic loafers and skimmer flats, jewelry is simple yet elegant, diamond post earrings, simple hoop earrings, simple tank watch, classic pearls, small splashes of color, classic scarves, simple makeup

- **Dramatic Fashion Personality:** trendy, always changing, bright bold colors, large shapes, mixing and matching patterns, new looks, comfort is secondary, high heel shoes, bold makeup, trendy shoes, bold jewelry, large colorful and detailed handbags, unusual outerwear, ever changing hair styles

- **Natural Fashion Personality:** simple lines, comfort is key, neutral colors, slacks, easy-to-wear tops and sweaters, jeans or chinos, comfortable shoes, loafers, jewelry to a minimum such as a watch and wedding ring or simple post earrings, minimal or no makeup, easy-care hair, ponytails, short hair

- **Sporty Fashion Personality:** favorite outfit is athletic wear, jog suits, sneakers, shorts, t-shirts, comfortable jeans or chinos teamed up with a sport logo t-shirt, no jewelry except a sports watch and wedding band, ball caps, makeup to a minimum such as lip gloss and mascara or no makeup, simple hair style

The descriptions given are examples of popular themes in dressing. People can choose clothing for many reasons. People may choose the same theme because they like the way the clothing fits their body. A particular style may make them confident and comfortable. Dressing with a common theme can project a pleasing picture.

Some individuals enjoy more than one fashion detail. They mix and match accessories successfully. An example would be: a classic fashion personality chooses tailored suits and structured silhouettes but also adds a touch of romance to her classic look with a brooch or a lace satin hankie in her jacket pocket.

The person just described favors a classic style as her primary fashion personality. She also enjoys hints of feminine touches, which are represented by the romantic fashion personality. This person has a secondary fashion personality.

A person can change her primary fashion personality for many reasons. The following are just some examples:

1. Leaving the work force

2. Moving to a new location

3. Becoming exposed to other tastes

4. Changing careers

5. Taking up a new hobby

6. Starting a new job

7. Limited budget

8. Changing figure

Now that you have some idea of your own fashion personality, sort through your clothing and see if your garments are expressing what you want them to. Do not forget to keep the main theme in mind when reviewing your accessories. Assess each item by asking the following questions:

• Does this item fit you and do you wear it?

• Do you feel good in this item and is it flattering to your body type?

• Does the item need repair or cleaning?

• Does it work with other items in your wardrobe?

• Do you wear this garment weekly, monthly, yearly?

• Do you have more than one of this item and why?

• Does this item represent the past and you can't part with it?

• Do you recognize your primary/secondary fashion personalities?

After completing the evaluation and having sorted through all items and placed them in the various categories, look at what you have in the repair, cleaning, throw away and giveaway areas. If anything in these areas requires replacement, write down the color and item. Try the items on in front of a mirror. This will help you to better evaluate how the clothing looks. After this portion is completed, decide what to do with each garment.

Make a choice regarding all items. After the bags, boxes, and containers have been filled, set them to the side. Look closely at any common themes that you see in your clothing selection. The common theme could be related to events or functions you attend. A specific silhouette may be what is repeated or it may be a certain type of fabric. Color is a very dominant characteristic that many people like repeating in their clothing. Besides color, people may have items of clothing that relate to something they do or places they go.

A single woman who works twelve-hour days, six days a week, may have little need for workout clothes.

If you are a person just re-entering the work force, you may not have clothes that are appropriate for your career. If you are just finishing school, your wardrobe may consist of jeans and t-shirts. Some other clothing categories that would reflect your activities could include the following:

• Work/Career dressing

• Casual weekend wear

• Formal attire and dressy clothes

• Jeans and sweatshirts/t-shirts

• Travel and vacation attire

• Yoga/workout

• Uniforms

• Vintage or keepsake clothing

The previous list can act as a guide to help define your clothing needs. The clothes that you own are now categorized into specific items, they are items that fit and work in your wardrobe at this time. You may also understand your lifestyle needs more clearly, as well as knowing your primary and secondary fashion personalities. Here are some questions to ask yourself:

1. Do you have the right items for your lifestyle needs?

2. Do you have several items in one category but are lacking in another?

3. Do you want to expand your primary and secondary fashion personalities?

4. Do you own too many clothes?

5. Do you enjoy your clothing?

6. Do your accessories work with your personal style?

7. Do you have the correct theme in both clothing and accessories?

After answering the questions above, you can plan your shopping list accordingly. Purchasing the needed items will allow for a more workable wardrobe. Another part of an organized wardrobe is the actual storage space.

Storage Space Assessment

Assessing your closet storage space will allow you to better use your wardrobe and utilize your clothing space appropriately. Understanding that you have too many clothes in a space will allow you to redefine that space by assigning a new home to specific items.

Storing off-season items in a secondary closet will free up space for the current season. The clothing will be less wrinkled because all the clothes will not be smashed together in a tight space. Ask yourself the following questions:

1. Do your clothing items fit into the primary space you use while dressing?

2. Can you see what you have with ease?

3. Can you slide things from side to side?

4. Are you hanging items that should be folded?

5. Do you store spring and summer items with fall and winter items?

Concentrate on the primary space you use in the morning and work with the current season. The clothing that you wear during the off-season should be in a secondary location.

Now that everything is out of your primary closet, you can start to organize this space. Begin by making sure that the items in your closet belong in this space. For example: are you storing books, craft items, sporting equipment, wrapping paper, photo albums, etc. in this space? Is this where you want to store these items? Can you store these items in a different location so you can utilize your closet more efficiently for your clothing? Make the decision now. This will help you as you begin to put your clothing items away.

As you start putting your clothing back into your closet, ask yourself how you want it organized. What is the best way for you? Some people sort clothing by item, some by color, and others by the outfit. By sorting your clothing by item, you can easily mix and match tops with bottoms. For this example, clothing will be organized by item and then by color within each category.

Begin by putting your clothing back into your closet as items have been lying on your bed or flat surface. You already have them sorted by item; pants with pants; shirts with shirts; skirts with skirts; etc. Hang the items from light to dark within the specific categories.

Depending on your closet style, walk-in or look-in, make sure that items that are seldom worn are to the back or to the far sides of your closet. If you can store off-season items in another closet or in plastic storage containers, do so. Clothing should be hung so that you can move the items from side to side on the rod. The following are some helpful storage tips:

Storage Tips

• Place frequently-used items front and center.

• Place shoes in clear plastic bins and label with: color, style, heel size.

• Add a second rod for short hanging items such as blouses and skirts.

• Utilize floor space and all shelf space to the fullest by adding dividers and utilizing shelf separators.

• Hang all items in the same direction using all the same hangers. Wooden hangers are a good choice.

• Use belt/tie/scarf hangers or store in clear plastic containers and label.

• Utilize all space in the closet by hanging items on hooks or adding shelves where needed. Don't forget to utilize the closet door.

Conclusion

Clothing and personal appearance are a mirror of how a person feels about herself while projecting an image to others. Wardrobe organization is an essential component that enables you to utilize your clothing and accessories fully. Take time to review and evaluate your clothing and accessories. Identify your fashion personality and create a wardrobe that meets your personal and professional needs. Collectively, these will be beneficial as you pursue your goal of achieving success in your professional career and personal life.

ABOUT THE AUTHOR

MYRTLE LOOBY

Myrtle Looby is President and Primary Consultant of LEAP Training Consultants, based in Antigua and Barbuda. She designs and conducts outstanding workshops and training seminars on a wide range of topics to diverse audiences throughout the Caribbean on such topics as Communication Skills and Women's Issues. In addition, she manages the Guidance and Learning Centre and is the president and Founder of Chrysalis-Antiguas/Barbuda, a non-profit organization which offers counseling, vocational and educational services to women.

Ms. Looby has had a successful career as a trained educator of English and Communication Skills in Trinidad, Tobago and Antigua (where she now resides). She is an advocate for lifelong learning. Her background and expertise, coupled with her wide experience working with adults, have contributed to the passion and dynamism that she brings to her workshops, seminars, and presentations.

One of her dreams has always been to become a published book author dealing with women's issues. She is currently working on her second publication.

Contact:
LEAP Training Consultants
P.O. Box W704
Wood's Centre
St. Johns, ANTIGUA
(268) 460-5504
guidance@candw.ag
www.protrain.net

FOURTEEN

MALE–FEMALE COMMUNICATION STYLES

By Myrtle Looby

*"Gender differences in communication are everywhere.
Once you start looking for them, you see them.
That awareness is the first step toward change."*
—*Dane Archer*

Do you remember the rhyme that says girls are made of sugar and spice and everything nice and boys are made of frogs and snails and puppy dogs' tails? This seemingly simple rhyme characterizes some of the differences in the roles males and females are expected to fulfill – females, as dainty little ladies who are always pleasant and sweet, and needed to make the main ingredients more palatable, while males, however unpleasant to some, have their own individuality.

At birth, most babies cry as they take their first gasp of air, with or without that proverbial slap. They all make the same noises and use their facial muscles to express pleasure, discomfort, relief or fright. Some of our non-verbal language acquired from birth is innate, such as crying,

157

smiling and chuckling, while as we grow and develop, we learn how to express ourselves verbally and non-verbally.

We communicate our feelings, attitudes and values by our tone of voice, rate of speech, language and vocabulary, movement, gestures and posture, and how we utilize the space around us. Our legs, hands, eyes and facial muscles speak volumes without our saying a word!

Throughout life, our learned patterns of communication are expressions of socially determined maleness or femaleness and our culture or sub-culture, ethnicity, age, class, and geographical location dictate these styles. The stereotypes are reinforced by our families, school, religion, peers, the media, and the workplace.

All males and females do not fit in the same mold but our upbringing, educational standard, level of self confidence, personal choice, and other considerations are critical factors in how we communicate. Take a look at those around you. Do you observe that males and females generally use their bodies in different ways to communicate? Listen to them speaking. Do you detect distinct differences?

There are far more similarities than differences but take the following fun quiz to test your awareness of the male/female differences in communication. You may want to discuss them with a friend or co-worker. Encircle either (m) or (f) to indicate whether you think that males or females display these characteristics more often than the other sex.

1. Use phrases like "sort of" or "kind of" when speaking
   This is called "hedging."   (f) (m)

2. Share more personal information in conversations   (f) (m)

3. Take more time when they have the floor at meetings   (f) (m)

4. Use tag questions, e.g., "You are the new sales rep., aren't you?" (f) (m)

5. Claim more personal space at the table with legs wide
   and documents slightly scattered
   (f) (m)

6. Are over-polite when making requests, by beginning with,
   "If you don't mind?" "If it is not too much trouble?" (f) (m)

7. Tend to cry openly (f) (m)

8. Tend to shout to get a point across (f) (m)

9. Use more swear words in conversations (f) (m)

10. Use their hands and eyes more when speaking (f) (m)

11. Ask questions like, "What do you think?" to build
    consensus, rather than make assertions (f) (m)

12. Interrupt 75 – 90% of the time (f) (m)

13. Talk more about their accomplishments (f) (m)

14. Use more fillers in speech like "er," "uh" (f) (m)

15. Speak at a slower rate and with a wider voice range (f) (m)

16. Maintain better eye contact during conversations (f) (m)

17. Say more "I'm sorry" in conversations when they are
    not really accepting blame (f) (m)

18. Give more jokes directed at others (f) (m)

19. Give more jokes directed at self, in a self-deprecating manner (f) (m)

20. Are more guilty of flaming i.e. publicly insulting someone
    when both are using an online service (f) (m)

Answers: 1(f), 2(f), 3(m), 4 (f), 5(m), 6(f), 7(f), 8(m), 9 (m), 10(f), 11(f), 12(m), 13(m), 14(f), 15(f), 16(m), 17(f), 18(m), 19(f), 20(m)

Similarities and Differences

We can all improve our communication skills to become more professional, but these stereotypical patterns are natural to most men and women. There is no right or wrong way to communicate, nor is any style superior to the other, but each has its strengths and brings variety to our discourse.

Miscommunication occurs when, based on our own perception of acceptable male/female communication styles, we ascribe certain meanings to verbal and non-verbal language, which may or may not be what was intended. The key is to acknowledge and understand the differences and similarities and expand our own styles to respond in ways appropriate to the situation.

Deborah Tannen, in her book *"You Just Don't Understand: Men and Women in Conversation"* claims that men use language to give and receive information and to compete. Their language is more direct and less emotional. They are generally more adept at issuing orders and fixing what they consider to be problems.

On the other hand, women communicate to build rapport. To women, conversation is interactive and fosters bonding. They self-disclose easily and openly with their "sister friends" and expect feedback. They empathize and suggest, instead of being direct. To them, relationships, intimacy and community are important.

Susan, in her early thirties, became the CEO of an ailing organization with a staff of thirty. She was self-confident, independent and took control. As a boss, these qualities served her well in revitalizing the organization and making a substantial profit. However, to her female employees, she was too bossy and unfeminine. To their male counterparts, she was a bitch! She had crossed the gender lines and deviated from the stereotype!

In the business and professional world, males are still more prevalent in positions of prestige and power and are the major decision-makers. Much of their communication style, both verbal and nonverbal, is geared towards establishing and maintaining their positions. They tend to take control, to compete and be more independent. Women's communication is more acceptable to men if it is less aggressive, and more passive and submissive.

The more self-confident women are the more assertively they communicate, and some males feel intimidated by their strength of character. To some female professionals, this may offer challenges and in a world where there may be a scarcity of women at the top, compliments and pats on the back can be few and far between.

Joanne, a new teacher on a predominately male staff, was put off when the male principal entered the staff room and made a request of her. He hardly glanced her way, looked around the room while he picked up a pencil from her desk and then left. Joanne would have preferred if he had addressed her by making eye contact and waited for her response before leaving. She found his behavior rude and the interaction impersonal and concluded that he did not like her. She later realized that that was his style of asserting himself with his staff. Experiences like these can be frustrating, especially to the young professional woman in a male- dominated workplace.

There are distinct conversational styles in same-sex interactions but we often make adjustments depending on the composition of the group. Do you remember when as children, girls would close the door when their girl friends came over, saying, "No boys allowed!" We are more comfortable communicating with our own sex as our scripts are generally the same. We are, more often than not, "on the same page."

Our all-female Reading Club would usually "hang out" on Friday nights, while our spouses would "wind down" at the neighborhood sports bar. We women looked forward to bringing one another up-to-date on the latest office scoop. We exchanged children stories and gave shopping tips. Husbands and significant others also came in for some "good tongue-lashing" in their absence. One night, our spouses joined us, and immediately our communication styles and content changed. Neither our spouses nor the ladies communicated in accustomed ways; but we automatically adjusted our styles. When the males joined, the communication style was more rambunctious. When the majority of us were women, then there was more "women talk."

Over a period of months, I made notes on the different patterns of communication displayed by males and females in an organization to which I belong. The following are lists of the female and male speech patterns identified.

Females:
• Use hedges like "kind of" and "sort of"

• Use tag questions like "You are the vice president, *aren't you?*"

• Use adjectives that are empty like "adorable" and "lovely"

• Speak with emphasis on words like "so" and "very" as in "I am so appreciative of....!"

• Are hypercorrect in pronunciation and grammar

• Use more words and give more detail that is often unnecessary

• Use more body language with hands, eyes and facial muscles

• Are overly polite in making requests like "If it is not too much trouble?"
• Are hesitant, using disclaimers such as "I don't know, but..."

• Take fewer and shorter turns when speaking at a meeting

• Use sentence fillers as "uhm" and "er"

Males:

• Use loud tone of voice and in a more assertive manner

• Take more and longer turns when speaking at a meeting

• Use more swear words in conversations

• Use metaphors about male body parts, e.g., testicular fortitude

• Demonstrate a more robust sense of humor

• Men's body language, e.g., wide gestures, knees spread apart utilizing more personal space, give the impression of status and dominance, by carving out larger personal space

• Interrupt more to get their point across

• Use conversational bantering to oppose and gain status in a group

• Paraphrase more by not providing many details

• Are unwilling to ask for directions and assistance or admit ignorance, in order to maintain status. The absence of necessary information impedes decision making and jeopardizes teamwork.

The Masks Women Wear

Being an authentic communicator builds trust and genuine relationships and lessens the chances of transmitting mixed or ineffective messages, but many women believe that they must assume different personalities or masks. These are some of the masks that are often used. Give examples of the verbal and non-verbal communication styles you think are associated with them:

• Ms. Prim and Proper:

• Ms. Ladylike:

• Ms. Martyr:

• Ms. Pity Me:

• Ms. Aggressive:

• Ms. Flirt:

• Ms. Go Along to Get Along:

• Ms. Overbearing:

• Ms. Complainer:

• Ms Perfect:

If you see yourself behind any of these masks, you may need the help of a trusted co-worker to assist you in making the necessary adjustments to be more true to yourself.

Communicating in Cyberspace

Here are some areas in which males and females communicate differently on the Internet:

• Choice of conversation topics

• Ways of speaking

• Use of emoticons

• Males are more guilty of flaming, sarcasm and harsh put-downs

In the absence of face-to-face contact and physical identification, much of the sex stereotyping in cyberspace communication is absent but the names you use on the internet are your identity and they do influence the type of interaction you have with others. Email addresses or names with a feminine ring sometimes attract inappropriate responses. Many organizations avoid this by assigning email addresses to their employees.

A young and talented self-employed graphic artist could not understand why her clients did not respond to her emails even after several reminders. She wondered if the fact that she was of a different ethnic group had anything to do with it. It was when she took a trip to one of the offices that she realized her mistake. Their computer systems would automatically send any email from a sexually suggestive address straight to their junk mail! She promptly got a new email address that was more professional and one that would promote her business.

Communication Tips for the Professional Woman

Here are some tips to avoid male/female misunderstandings in the workplace.

• In conversations, aim at keeping the other person interested and engaged. Be sensitive. Conversations about job-related issues, topical events and non-personal matters are more appropriate for the work-place. Talking to men about your personal experiences may send the wrong message. You may feel the need to bond with your female co-workers by discussing personal matters, but do so within limits. Be wary of office gossip. Once your secrets are out, they are out of your control.

• Men tend to be more comfortable speaking or writing about their accomplishments than women do. Your male co-workers will be more interested in your accomplishments and what you plan to do than in how you feel about a situation.

• Some women consider speaking of accomplishments to be boasting or bragging. Consequently, many women fail to "blow their own trumpet" and end up not promoting or marketing themselves enough. Women who downplay their accomplishments become vulnerable to a more assertive or aggressive "competitor" and may be passed over for a position.

• Women complain that their ideas and suggestions are often ignored at meetings while the same ideas are later acknowledged and praised when they are repeated by a man. Practice speaking confidently, with a lower-pitched, well-modulated voice without over-enunciating your words, and use it to your professional advantage.

• Men generally interrupt women more than they do men. Women interrupt men less than they do women. Sometimes women's silence is taken as disinterest or their being out of their league, but women just take more time to listen to other opinions before giving theirs. Politely claim your turn to speak when you choose to and do not allow anyone to interrupt you.

• To achieve intimacy and interaction, women usually go into great detail to explain situations. Quite often, neither clients nor co-workers are impressed. Skip the details and get to the point! In addition, men tend to think that you are asking them to solve a problem when you are just talking it out.

• Avoid tagging, hedging, and the use of weak and empty adjectives and qualifiers. They may be ideal in friendships and intimate relationships but in business relationships, a more direct and assertive style is more appropriate.

- It is necessary to learn the jargon associated with your job. This is not a language reserved for some and using the language brings the team closer and makes communication more effective.

- Being overly polite and apologetic by saying "I'm sorry," when you are not wrong, expresses empathy, but it often makes you sound powerless. Make your requests and responses simple, straightforward and direct.

- In an attempt to gain consensus, women tend to include others in decision making. They want to discuss an issue before making a decision. More often than men, they ask "What do you think?" When women are consultative, it can be interpreted as being tentative, indecisive, and unassertive, time wasting and not utilizing their personal power. In spite of this, try to be decisive and think things through with greater urgency.

- Be certain that you are communicating the correct message when you keep nodding to a male speaker. He may feel that you are in agreement when you are just indicating that you are listening.

- When women ask questions, they may just do so to keep the conversation going. When men hear a question, they often provide unsolicited information. Don't get offended. Remember, they have a different script.

- Men generally love to banter and give jokes directed at others as they jostle for status and power within the group. Women may feel uncomfortable in such settings, and may even take the jokes as personal affronts. At the same time, accepting sexist and offensive jokes, swearing and rude comments is demeaning your own self-worth and would not make you "one of the guys."

- Having a sense of humor is an asset but neither you nor others should be the brunt of insensitive jokes. In addition, women's jokes are often self-directed and self-deprecating, as they make fun of their own mistakes in a diminishing manner. This depreciates their self-worth and is an indication of low self-esteem. Avoid drawing attention to your own problems and areas that need improvement. Remember, you do not need to devalue yourself to fit in.

- Sarcastic comments and "one-up-man" jokes are a part of the male-dominated work world. If you are not comfortable with them, say so firmly and politely, but do not react negatively by reprimanding or deriding.

- Assert yourself at meetings. If you can stand, move around. Claim the space around you. Make yourself comfortable and relaxed. Let your appearance, posture, speech, and gestures demonstrate self-confidence and power.

- Be flexible. Be prepared to make last-minute adjustments in emergencies. Never let them unnerve you, even under pressure! Women tend to become emotional in these settings, but don't act bothered. There are days when everything that can go wrong will go wrong, but those, too, shall pass. Stay focused and positive.

- It's certainly not "cute" to cry in a professional setting. Excuse yourself and use the washroom.

• Although women are moving up the corporate ladder and they are making inroads in traditional male domains, the playing field is not yet level. Take verbal rejection and negative feedback objectively. Don't take it personally and get defensive if challenged. It's not about you!

• Be aware of your facial expressions and use them to your advantage. A pleasant, relaxed smile coupled with eye contact makes you approachable. Be aware that there may be some cultural differences; in some Eastern cultures, females are not encouraged to make eye contact with the opposite sex or with their elders.

Awareness is the key

Being aware of, and adaptable to, the different communication styles that bring increased respect and remove obstacles to effective communication, is the key.

ABOUT THE AUTHOR

WILLIE JOE VARY

Willie Joe Vary, teacher, facilitator, educational consultant, and staunch advocate of personal empowerment to reach new heights, inspires students of all kinds. Joe Vary holds an M. Ed. and Rank I in teaching and certifications in Diversity Training, Facilitator Training, Leadership, and Communication Skills Training. Pursuing her first love—teaching—spanned over three decades. At the time of her "graduation," Willie Joe Vary had directed young minds in public school in grades one through eight. It was also during this period that she served on many boards of directors. Jefferson County Public School awarded her the coveted ExCel Award for teachers, Human Relations Award and a Life-time Member Award for PTA. A highlight in her career came with a standing ovation given at Mercy Academy, a private girl's school where she provided the keynote.

"There is star potential in all of us." Truly believing this led to the development of J. Vary & Associates, LLC. Her workshops and seminars are results oriented and utilize the latest in adult learning strategies.

Joe Vary has provided training experiences for the Professional Woman Network, where she serves on the International Advisory Board. Her most sought-after seminar had its beginning with The Professional Woman Network but has now been conducted for cancer survivors. Social and professional groups have also benefited from the very popular "Write To Life," journal-writing workshop. St. Stephen Church's women leadership team requested Joe's Goal-Setting Seminar. Several collaborative ventures with the Parker Group, LLP are planned.

Joe married her high school sweetheart, Marion Vary, and they have two daughters, Nicole and Marva. Marva and husband Trent have two children, Trent, Jr. and Ragan Marie. They are all members of St. Stephen Church in Louisville, Kentucky.

Contact:
J. Vary & Associates
8701 Lantern Lite Pkwy
Louisville, KY 40220
(502) 491-9738
jvassociates@bellsouth.net
www.jvassociates.org
www.protrain.net

FIFTEEN

JOURNALING FOR PERSONAL AND PROFESSIONAL ENRICHMENT

By Willie Joe Vary

Nights seldom brought more than four hours sleep and my weight ballooned to an unspeakable number. Doctor visits increased and many weekends were used only to finish household tasks or study/prepare for the coming week. Work was not a passion but just a job. What was wrong? How did I find myself without a title or a descriptor? Where are the joys and the passion I once knew and the total fulfillment of being "Marva's mom?" How long has it been since I heard, "Hi, are you Nikki's mother?" I didn't know what it was, but I did know it didn't feel good.

A quote by Tony Robbins repeatedly worked its way into my brain. "The quality of one's life is directly related to the quality of questions you ask yourself." Many questions and several journals later, I had my answer: "Empty nest." Now that I had a name for my crisis, what would I do about it? The answer to that and other questions lay between the pages of my journal. It was my job to ask them and write to a life that was truly worth living.

Why do people journal?

Often a journal is started in times of crisis. A new milestone, a life marker, or an "aha" moment will send one running to the journal. There are many times a happy event motivates the writer to begin journaling. The reasons are as varied as the individual. Many medical personnel recommend this activity to patients as a tool in the psychological healing practice. Gain personal insight, put thoughts, dreams and goals in order, to record family history . . .

> *September 2003*
> *M went to the playground with TJ and Ragan. Ragan was in the carrier. It was after school and Mom went to give them some wind down time. The idea was, if TJ could run and play and use up some of his energy, he would ease into a better bedtime routine. "Come TJ, let's go," was Mom's directive after about an hour of play. He wouldn't come and when she went after him, he ran farther from her. Limitations: She couldn't run after him because she had to pick up the carrier and run with Ragan. Results: TJ won and thus came a new concept – "put on your listening ears." What other "area" will need to be renamed? They will love this story.*

> *January 4, 2003*
> *Saturday morning was gym time but they didn't open. The gym was closed. Everyone went to Papa's house. They ate cereal, kool aid, and turkey hash. They tried out their new skates inside and it*

was decided that TJ's were too large and needed to be returned. Destroying MeMaw's lower right foot had nothing to do with the decision. We talked about conflict. TJ understands this abstract concept and our mission is to point out conflict and talk about how to solve it. Both of the children are happy, well, full and rested. My oldest leaves at 1:45 to go to the skating rink. This is pure joy watching your oldest child. How much of me do I see? What legacy am I leaving?

Providing a record for weight and health issues are also worthy uses of the journal. Some people use journals to record special prayers and events. A recent survey revealed a new and exciting use of the journal. Business leaders have brought the journal into the boardroom. Is this a hobby or does journal writing truly lead to personal and professional development? The story shared from the personal life of the writer clearly demonstrates the motivation emotional pain plays in beginning the journal. A journal does allow one to gain insight into the more challenging experiences of betrayal, loss and separation, as well as the ins and outs of building self-esteem.

The journey to personal development does not always begin with a negative. It can begin with a simple question "Who am I—really?" This is the best and most important place to begin the journey to personal development. The magazine writers and editors, talk-show hosts and close friends invite their audiences to become authentic, develop good relationships with money, peers, and the "inner child." All are good reasons to begin a journal. A desire to analyze the healing process, discover true meaning, live on purpose, obtain self-fulfillment, capture the true essence of happiness, prosperity and spirituality have all motivated the start of many journeys.

Journal writing empowers you to access your own inner power, uncovers roadblocks to you becoming your best, and provides an outlet to release stress.

> *Sister Girl Journal*
> *1. Is "fat" bad?*
> *There are two problems with fat. The big one is health. Fat creates problems for the heart, and other vital organs. Many people are in life threatening situations because of their fat. Activity is limited and fat causes stress on joints and several serious illnesses. Fat makes me tired and listless. It acts as a prisoner. Fun outdoor games are not a part of a fat person's life (me). The second problem with being fat is cosmetic. I can't wear the kind of clothes I want to wear. My body image is not the one I am happy with. This is not how I want to look. I want to wear tight jeans, halter tops, slim and sleek clothes. I want to look sexy and exciting.*

People journal because they want to be entertained, comforted, enlightened and organized. Many famous historical figures were journalers: Ben Franklin, Albert Einstein and Leonardo da Vinci. Perhaps the most well-known media figure of contemporary times, Oprah Winfrey, is an avid journaler. Her web site devotes an entire section to journaling.

The type of journal is as varied as the individual. "Keeping a journal will change your life in ways that you'd never imagine,"—Oprah.

Are there special tools for journaling?

Tools can be as simple as a plain notebook and pen or pencil. But since this is the beginning of a journey that will have but one passenger—YOU, spend some time and select materials you have a special response to. There are many beautiful leather and clothbound books to hold recordings of your journey. Bookstores and "dollar stores" devote entire sections to aid in the selection. A computer is certainly not required, but there are programs to fill the needs of the journalers who want to use the computer. There are many free and low-cost sites to encourage the beginner and the more confident writer. A journaler's list may look like this:

• Journal
• Pen/pencil
• Markers
• Crayons
• Colored pencils
• A three-ring binder and paper
• Computer
• Prompts: poems, quotes, the Bible and other personal choices
• A real desire to begin this journey to self-discovery

This step is all about selecting what is appealing to you. Do you like the feel of a soft leather journal or would a small hardcover with a Japanese theme on the front cover be more inviting to you? Many have reported their interest was sustained by writing on the computer. There are even computer programs and software for those who feel a need to work with technology. The journal is your book, written by you, for you and you alone. It can be whatever you want it to be. If it is your choice, then it's the right choice.

What should you do if you keep buying pretty books and you don't know what to write in them?

Many have gathered the items listed above and nothing happened. I would invite you to look at the last item on the list, "a real desire to begin the journey to self discovery." This is key to becoming a journaler. There are only two things you must do to unlock the wonderful, powerful forces that live inside of you. There are only two things you need to do to explore emotional healing, develop your mind, your spirituality, and your natural talents and live on purpose. They are #1: Believe it can happen, and #2: Start writing. Keep the list handy, do the two steps, and everything else you need will appear. If you still need support, enroll in a class, go out online, or contact me.

> *Yes, I was convinced what I had was the empty nest syndrome. But what do I do about it? The Tony Robbins quote was a real motivator. But now I have a cheap journal (mistake one), a pen and a quiet place to write. I didn't buy a journal that reflects the important commitment you are making to yourself. Nothing happened. Where were the answers? It had been easy writing to Dear Diary, as a teen love-struck kid. I didn't need to tell "the book friend" the ups and downs of my day like I did several decades ago. Gone was the need to answer, "who likes who?" and make a list of my favorite clothes. Now is a time for the teacher to "teach herself." What did I instruct my students to do?*

The best thing about writing in your journal is you don't need to worry about spelling, grammar, and a right or wrong way. Just write and be honest. I instructed my students to make lists identifying their best school activity. I also wrote lists. "Things I am grateful for" was the subject for days. "Things I like to do" gave me the push I needed to get more words on the blank pages. And before I knew it, certain themes and concepts seemed to leap off the page. The journal was bringing clarity to an otherwise foggy life.

There was "a friend at the end of the pen, which you can use to help you solve personal and business problems, get to know all the parts of yourself, explore your creativity… and much more," states Kathleen Adams, in her book, *Journal to the Self.*

Making lists is a perfect way to begin a journal. It gets words on paper and often that is just the hurdle you need to leap over to overcome the blank page syndrome. List makers are the taskmasters in running a business and their personal life. Sample pages might look like this:

List A: Things I would do if I had no limitation

List B: How would I spend ___amount of money

List C: Life's lessons

List D: Prayers

List E: Deadlines for home and work

List F: Books to read

List G: Why am I sad?

List H: What are my marketplace skills?

List I: Innovative projects

Look over your lists and, if none of them cause a slight reaction, continue making your list of lists. But by this time certain lists will create a reaction. The list will often provide the topic for the journal. Start with that list first. Highlight the list items that cause strong feelings. Select one and write it on a page, date it, and begin to ask yourself several questions. The tried and true "W Questions" work well here: Who, What, When, Where, Why, and How. "What is the most important job I have?" my friend, Hazel Parker, Chapter 24, would suggest you ask yourself. "Are you spending time on the things that are important to you? And what is keeping you from doing what you love to do?" Reflect on your day, your week or last year. Write about the highs and the lows and the accompanying feelings. Talk to the journal about your challenges. Let your mind clear, be still and just breathe. Now begin to write. Remember, self-awareness is fundamental to personal and professional growth. Repeat: Fundamental to personal growth and professional development is self-awareness.

It is at this point a personal contract would be very helpful. Write it on a page by itself.

I_____(your name) do solemnly promise to be brutally honest with my journal and write about my feelings, thoughts, hopes, dreams and challenges at least _____ time(s) a week. I will focus on the power within.

Sign_____

Wheel of Life
Ideal

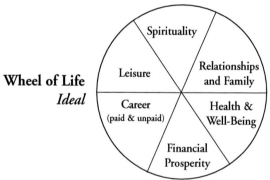

I invite you to look at
Stacey Vicari's "Wheel of Life."
Start by giving yourself permission to write about the importance of each of these in your life. Take the pie one section at a time. Write a section on a page and again, get still, reflect, breathe and write. Think about each section as "My Spirituality," "My Career," and so on. Create a clear picture

of spirituality, or your work. Are my relationships satisfying? Why? Why not? Clear your mind, get still, breathe and write. Spend some time with the "Financial Prosperity" slice. What are your investment goals? Finish this sentence "Financial prosperity is..." Write so that you may begin to understand how you would like your money to work for you. In your vision write what you see, feel, taste and the sounds of your vision. How can you make this vision a reality? Each time you write take another section. Ask yourself "Is my time spent on the things that are important to me?"

Who should journal?

All of that seems easy enough. Purchase a pretty book, make lists and take your cues from the power generated by making lists. Lists organize and motivate their owners to plan, solve problems and clear out the clutter, both physically and mentally. But several questions still remain about journal writing. Who should journal? Is it just a hobby? Does it require certain skill?

Journal writing is an activity for the rich and the poor, mothers and fathers, the CEO, entrepreneur and the project manager. Many seniors use the journal as a legacy for their grandchildren. Writing for personal and professional growth is for the receptionists at the front desk, planners and dreamers, and anyone who wants to know the most important person in your life—you. Oprah does it. Valerie Burton, author of *Listen to Your Life*, does it. Dr. Phil, eminent talk-show host, suggests it. Cheryl Richardson's *Take Time For Your Life*, a 7-step program for creating the life you want, would put all of your hard work in one document—your journal. Research continues to investigate the effects of writing in the healing process. People who write about traumatic events experience an improved sense of well-being. A healthcare worker engaged the journaler in a similar conversation.

Yes, I believe journal writing can be a very powerful, supplemental tool in the battle with many of our "health" enemies. "Will you share some of your activities and thoughts on the subject with a group of cancer survivors," was a question from a field healthcare worker. An oncologist was interested in having some of his patients engage in journal writing. The training was set for an evening and notices were posted and on the coldest night of the year, 27 people showed up. The group was composed of patients in treatment, survivors and caregivers. Most had little, if any, experience in writing. The group responded to the exercises immediately and with some encouragement and the use of several prompts started their first journal. Their first session began with an orientation and an identification of support systems, successes, and a chance to talk.

Other workshops have been given for those wanting to use journal writing in their fight for life. Sessions allow for reflection, meditation, and a time to talk to the "friend at the end of your pen." Margie Davis, The Healing Way says, "The journal is your intimate and confidential companion to use as you wish." How did the participants give closure to that workshop?

"I want to make tonight the beginning of my road to recovery…"
"I now know I need a support system and to put myself first more…"
"I am glad I came —my son is, too. It's like having a trusted friend."

Any woman who works in the business community realizes personal assessment of her skill sets, leadership styles, and her ability to see the big picture are critical for success in global competition. The journal moves into the boardroom. If you manage projects, people, teams or your time, journal writing is a tool for you. The business community is shifting more and more to bringing people together to work on single projects and assigning project leaders. Can a project leader use a journal? A list of one current project leader looks like this:

• Planning	• Analyzing
• Scheduling	• Facilitating
• Recruiting	• Assessing
• Negotiating	• Communicating
• Budgeting	• Delegating
• Coaching	• Team building

M: Help! I need one tool to help me keep it all together. I was just given the most coveted project in the company. What should I do?

J: Let's design a journal for the project manager. Taking the journal into the boardroom requires a special format.

Paramount to leadership is the ability to prioritize, manage, and see the big picture. An effective leader has a winning game plan and that plan starts before the meeting. It is at this point that a "talk to the friend at the end of the hand" is beneficial. Create a time to write about each of the items below. Make this your regular activity and watch productivity soar. The following is an example:

• Goals/vision/mission

• List jobs/responsibilities

• My inventory of leadership skills

• Guiding questions

• Obstacles and opposition

Some of the questions M came up with at the onset were:

1. How do you motivate people?

2. Ways to win team-commitment, team-trust and respect.

3. How to create an environment to foster productivity?

4. How to build a creative factor? What are the risks?

5. What are my strengths and weaknesses?
   What are the strengths and weaknesses of my team members?

6. An audit of my team and the company reveals...

7. An audit of the tasks reveals...

8. Books I need to read

The entrepreneur must concern herself with management, money, marketing, and service. Answering certain questions in a journal, where they can be reviewed and used to create an action plan, is a worthy habit to begin. Turning bad situations into productive, profitable exchanges is a strategy the entrepreneur must utilize. Focusing on interpersonal skills is as crucial in the workplace as wearing the correct attire. The journal can be invaluable in logging data and recording information that produces insight and is there for the next big project.

Management
1. What are weaknesses?
2. What support people do I need to devote more time to?
3. My reward system:

Money
1. How must our resources be allocated?
2. What steps can be taken to increase cash flow?
3. What affects profits?

Marketing

1. Where are networking opportunities?
2. What is my niche?
3. How can I improve sales and service?

Service

1. How do we cater to our customers?
2. How do we show we are committed to our program?
3. How do we share our knowledge?

Project leaders and business owners alike must keep in the forefront of what they are trying to accomplish (Goals), when the job needs to be completed (Timeframe), what impedes progress (Risks), how much money or how many people are needed to complete this project (Resources) and who is impacted by this project (Effects). The journal is a natural for the boardroom.

Journaling can be and may start as a hobby, but like many hobbies, journaling can turn into something life-altering. Paradigm shifts have started from the pages of a journal. Yes, it is very effective if you want to get in touch with your inner-self, find and protect your inner-child, and become the beautiful person you were created to be. It would be a pity to answer the call of the journal only in times of anxiety, sadness and despair or keep it out of the boardroom.

Let's not forget the value of journaling for the teacher. The journal is a tool to facilitate learning, begin class, and provide documentation for the grade. Reading and English teachers use this tool regularly but other teachers may also find this tool useful. Prompts can be inserted in the beginning of the lesson to settle down the class. The middle of the lesson is a good place to use prompts to check for understanding, maintain learning and ensure that you have active learners. Every lesson must end with a good closure.

Before the lesson:

1. Write what you know about_____.

2. How does this topic relate to _____?

3. What problem are you having with this topic?

Break in the lesson:

1. Write several things you have learned.

2. What question do you have now?

3. How do you feel about this lesson?

As a closure activity:

1. How could this lesson have been better?

2. What was good about this lesson?

3. How involved was I in this lesson?

Teachers are not the only group that can use these questions. Parents, in place of "What did you do today?" when your son or daughter comes home from school, try one of the "teacher" questions. If you jot down the answers, it gives the child a sense of how important you feel her answers are. Where would you put the answers? In a journal, of course

Is there another way a journal can be used by two people?

A couple that wants to really get to know each other could certainly create a "Couples Journal." Challenges in both love and marriage occur when one or both fail to live up to the expectations of the other. This suggests there is no real partnership. A couple's journal engages both parties in sharing, reflecting and expressing their expectations. Set aside a time for both of you to go over and commit to the process. Decide on a different color for each respondent. Go over the "All About Me Questions." Put the journal in a certain place and agree on a time to share each other's reflections. The questions below suggest several prompts for the couple that wants to begin developing a solid partnership where expectations are in the open. Use them as a beginning and relax and explore the making and maintaining of the partnership.

"All About Me" Questions

• Write your name and decorate it with colors etc. Where did your name come from?

• Who is your role model and why? What connection do you feel to that person?

• What things do you like to do after work and on weekends? Do you prefer a group or solitary activity?

• Are friends important to you? Who is your best friend and why?

• Explore money, family, children, and time management.

• Reflect and write about spirituality.

• Name your ideal career and tell why.

• What things are you good at doing?

• How do you become the best of the best?

Journaling to personal and professional development is a journey you begin because your friend does it, a talk show host does it, your favorite author suggests it, or you were given a journal for your birthday. Try it and see what a truly powerful tool the "little friend at the end of your hand" becomes. The friend is there regardless of what hat you wear: entrepreneur, project leader, spouse, teacher, healer, or writer. Close your eyes, take several deep breaths, reflect, put on a hat and begin to write.

ABOUT THE AUTHOR

ROSEMARY BONILLA

Rosemary Bonilla currently resides in Staten Island, New York with her husband and two children aged twenty and thirteen. She has over twenty years experience in the healthcare industry with ten years at a management level and is currently pursuing a Master's Degree in Health Administration. She has taught Medical Billing/Coding at Wagner College in Staten Island, New York. Ms. Bonilla is president and CEO of a profitable medical billing company, president and CEO of a real estate holding company, as well as a practice manager for the Department of Radiology at Maimonides Medical Center.

She holds memberships with the New York State Real Estate Association, National Association of Female Executives, Radiology Business Management Association, Medical Group Management Association, New Day Toastmasters, Fellow in the American College of Medical Practice Executives, and is an International Advisory Board member of The Professional Woman Network.

Rosemary Bonilla is a Certified Trainer in personal and professional development and conducts seminars and workshops nationally and internationally specializing in developing a positive self-image, financial freedom and personal and professional development. She is also available for personal and professional coaching sessions.

Contact:
Rosemary Bonilla
Faculty Practice Manager
Radiology Department
Maimonides Medical Center
4802 Tenth Avenue
Brooklyn, NY 11219
(718) 283-6157
rbonilla@maimonidesmed.org
www.protrain.net

SIXTEEN

OVERCOMING NEGATIVITY

By Rosemary Bonilla

As I am writing this story I am filled with emotion. It is very difficult for me to write. This story is about my mother. She was a vibrant, healthy, beautiful, talented and loving woman who had a great fear of being alone. My older sister and I left our mother's home at a very young age, which left my little sister, who has Down's Syndrome, at home. My mother constantly spoke about the way she was going to die. For years she would say how she would die suddenly and because there would be no one to help her, she surely would perish. At the age of fifty-two (and without warning) my mother suddenly collapsed on her living room floor from an aneurysm in her brain that burst. My little sister tried to call my older sister but could not dial her telephone number correctly. The next day my older sister found my mother on the floor hardly breathing. She was rushed to the hospital but it was too late. My mother died three days later. Not a day goes by that I do not recall my mother's beautiful smile, her warm embrace or her laughter. We all miss her terribly as she was the core of our family.

I am telling you this story *because you must be careful how to you talk to yourself, as the words shape your world.*. We must consciously be aware and acknowledge our self-talk and our conversations with others for they will often impact our future. Every human being is a prophet. We affect our future with our thoughts, words and actions. But your thoughts are the first step in predicting your future. Your thoughts are like seeds planted in the ground; ultimately they will spring forth either to bloom and become flowers, or grow and become weeds. Henry Ford said it best:"If you think you can, you can!"

In order to overcome negative behaviors we must first identify and internalize the true meaning of positive behaviors. I would like you to get out your pen, look up the meaning of every word you find below and write the meaning on the blank line next to it. Positive behaviors are brought about through a positive self-image belief system, which is directly connected to love, hope and faith. They are as follows:

Compassion: _____

Joy: _____

Patience: _____

Persistence: _____

Purpose: _____

Courage: _____

Expectancy:_____

Gratitude: _____

Self-worthiness:_____

Wisdom: _____

Confidence: _____

Happiness:_____

Now really study the meaning of these words, dwell on them and internalize them. These should be your dominating thoughts, which in turn will become your behavior.

We will also have to recognize the true meaning of negative behaviors. Again, please look up the meaning of these words and write them down next to the blanks. Negative behaviors are brought about through a negative self-image belief system, which is directly connected to fear and doubt. They are as follows:

Blame: _____

Depression: _____

Anxiety: _____

Indifference: _____

Judgement: _____

Indecision: _____

Procrastination: _____

Perfectionism: _____

Resentment: _____

Jealousy: _____

Envy: _____

Self-pity: _____

Confusion: _____

Guilt: _____

These negative words should not be our main thoughts and behaviors. (Of course, from time to time these words will pop into our minds, but we should stop them before we start behaving negatively.) We can stop them with positive thoughts and eventually will bring forth positive behaviors.

There is a universal law, which is the law of action and reaction. The action is your thought and the reaction is the response of your subconscious mind. Your mind is your most precious possession. You think with your conscious mind and whatever you habitually think sinks down to your subconscious mind, which then creates according to the nature of your thoughts. So think about it! You have the power to create your world. The belief of your mind is simply the thought of your mind. Therefore, I want you to write down what you believe about yourself. Write down all positive beliefs you have about yourself. (You can reference the positive behavior words that you looked up on the preceding page.)

_____

_____

_____

_____

_____

_____

_____

_____

_____

_____

_____

_____

_____

Now concentrate on these positive beliefs about yourself. Make these affirmations about yourself and concentrate on them daily. When you can do this exercise every day and think of the person you plan to become, you will create in your mind a clear mental picture of a positive self-image of yourself. You will be utilizing creative imagination. *You* be the change that you wish to see in the world. Believe that through the principal of self-acceptance of this belief of yourself and positive self-affirmations, this positive self-image will become your desire, which will ultimately become reality.

What you persistently hold in your mind will eventually seek expression through some practical means of obtaining what you need. Therefore, take ten minutes daily to develop and demand confidence in yourself. Faith is the starting point for all accumulation of riches. Many people are closed off to their own potential because they do not know about the storehouse of infinite intelligence and boundless love within themselves. They are constantly looking externally as a solution to their problems instead of internally. You must look within yourself "for whatever you want, you can draw forth." There are people who are full of confidence and faith. These people know they are born to succeed and they expect it. Do not be full of fear and doubt, as ultimately, this fear to go forward will make you simply stay where you are.

It is up to you to decide what you really want out of life. It is your responsibility. Write down anything that you have ever wanted to do, become or possess. Remember the shortest pencil is better than a long memory. These goals can be spiritual, physical, mental, financial, or family related. Choose the top three goals from this list and write down at least five actions you can do now toward accomplishing these "big three" priority goals. A big success is simply several little successes linked together. Be alert to the opportunities and people who will come into your life because of your positive self-image belief system. Keep and write in a journal.

My top three goals:

1._____

_____

2._____

_____

3._____

_____

Action plan for achieving my goals:

1._____

_____

2._____

_____

3._____

_____

4._____

_____

5._____

_____

Remember it is not what others say about you that really matters in life. It is what you believe about yourself. Successful people believe in themselves. They stay focused and have good character. But remember not every person likes successful people. There will always be a critic. You must never allow what others say about you to change your opinion of yourself, NEVER. People will always fight what they do not understand. The mind will always resent what it cannot master. Keep focused and persistent on your positive self-image and goals. Know your skills, talents and abilities. Everyone has gifts, EVERYONE. Do what you love to do. If you cannot recognize your skills, talents and abilities ask your relatives and friends what they feel may be your gifts.

Four ways to find your gifts:
1. Do what you love to do.
2. Do what your family and friends think you do well.
3. Ask yourself: who are your heroes or people you most admire? What do they do?
4. Volunteer for some cause that is dear to your heart.

When you serve others, your skills, talents and abilities are bound to come out. Money is merely a reward for solving problems and serving others. When we concentrate on our service to others, we are truly doing what we were meant to do. Your attitude will reflect your success. Eliminate all negative self-image beliefs about yourself. Not everyone is perfect and we all have strengths and weaknesses, but you should focus on your strengths, skills, talents and abilities.

Focus on the good in others and the world. Be grateful and count your blessings and be willing to make mistakes, for through them we grow and learn that they too are blessings. Eliminate hatred, envy, jealousy, cynicism and fear of failure by developing love for all humanity. Realize and believe that a negative attitude toward yourself and others can never bring you success. People decide their habits and their habits decide their future. A negative attitude is just that: a habit.

I would like to discuss mental pictures and creative imagination. We have two parts to our brain. The left side of the brain holds logic, facts, figures, and analysis. The right side of the brain holds concepts, emotions, images, and sensations. The right side of your brain unleashes your creative imagination power. You can stimulate your creative imagination with the use of mental imagery. Your creative imagination is the part of your brain where all great ideas are captured. You must develop this part of your brain with the following:

• Altering to positive input
• Rational mental exercise
• Blocking out distractions
• Relaxation
• Resisting interference from the left side of the brain
• Replaying relevant past successes
• Mental imagery of peak performance

When you develop mental imagery of how you imagine your life to be in your mind, you can program your mind to create these images through your positive self-image belief system with positive thoughts and positive affirmations, which will produce positive behaviors, habits and attitude. That is why meditation is very important in developing your creative imagination. Imagine yourself as the successful person you plan to become; believe that you are this person and when you close your eyes for three minutes a day, see yourself being this person.

When a negative thought comes into your mind (since these thoughts may have been your dominating thoughts) you will have to work on letting them go by saying to yourself "Stop!" and dwell on positive thoughts, positive people or a positive situation. It takes approximately twenty-one days for a habit to form, so be patient and know that it may take twenty-one days to break the habit of negative thoughts and behaviors.

Ten Ways to Overcome Negative Thoughts:
1. Focus on the good things in your life and expect the best to happen.
2. Consistently cultivate a positive outlook of life itself.
3. Do not put excessive value on money, but put value on serving others.
4. Believe how important you are to your family, friends and community.
5. Do not dwell on feeling like a victim. Find solutions to your problems.
6. Remember that you are equal to all others.
7. Control your anger.
8. Do not ignore the feelings and rights of others. Have empathy.
9. Practice forgiveness.
10. Let go of self-pity.

Remember that to succeed, you must examine three major characteristics, as they will set the course of your life:

Your beliefs: They set the course of your life and are the captain of your ship. Your world will carry the orders of the captain. Set your course toward positive land.

Your attitude: This is determined by your beliefs (thoughts) and how you feel about the past, future, self and others.

Your actions: These are what you are doing to achieve your goals to complete the journey you have set.

A belief is a thought in your mind. Do not believe in things that will harm or hurt you. Believe in the power of your subconscious to heal, inspire, strengthen, and prosper you. Use your mind to bless, heal and inspire people everywhere. You have the power to choose how you will react to the suggestions of others. Believe in good fortune and expect it, along with abundance and the blessings of life. According to your belief (thought) so it is done to you. Change your thoughts and you will change your destiny.

You have the power.

Notes:

ABOUT THE AUTHOR

MYRALYN STEWART MILLER

Myralyn Stewart Miller, CEO and President of the Stewart Miller Communication Institute for Excellence, is a speech pathologist, educator and entrepreneur. Myralyn Miller received a Bachelor of Arts Degree in French Liberal Arts and a Master of Arts degree in Speech Pathology with a minor in Linguistics. Extensive studies were in the areas of supervision, administration, leadership, speech pathology and accent reduction.

Myralyn Miller is an ASHA-certified and -licensed speech pathologist who works extensively with children, youths and adults addressing communication disorders and dysphagia. She has conducted numerous workshops and in-services for parents, staff, peers, educators, and administrators relative to speech and language development, vocal abuse behaviors, accent reduction programs and swallowing issues.

As an entrepreneur, Myralyn Miller offered continuing education programs as a Florida provider for healthcare professionals. In her free time, she develops speech therapy games, activities, and products. Beginning summer 2005, she will offer intensive camp programs focusing on Fast ForWord, social interactions, etiquette skills, speech improvement, language learning, and accent enhancement. Myralyn served as board advisor for the Port Gibson Mental Health Center in Mississippi and is an International Advisory Board Member of The Professional Woman Network.

Myralyn Stewart Miller wishes to thank her parents and her husband, training consultant John Miller, Jr. for their assistance with this book.

Myralyn Miller, MA-CCC-SLP

Contact:
Myralyn Miller, MA, CCC-SLP
Stewart Miller Communication Institute for Excellence
(904) 537-3629
myralyn@stewartmillercommunication.com
www.stewartmillercommunication.com

SEVENTEEN

COMMUNICATE TO WIN

By Myralyn Stewart Miller

Let's build bridges, not walls
—Martin Luther King

Communication is at the core of all exchanges, whether formal or informal, personal or professional, technical or non-technical. The ability to get a point across is important for information, persuasion, entertainment or personal involvement. The way you use words for speaking or writing, as well as the tone of voice you use for conveying information will impact your business and personal relationships. Communicating thoughts and emotions and working through conflict requires skill in speaking, listening and assertion. The skill you display will have a direct bearing on the quality of your inter-personal relationships at work and at home.

EXERCISE 1: Communication Self-Assessment
Complete the self-assessment about your communication ease by placing an X in the box corresponding to the statement. Review your answers and take a

moment to reflect on your completed assessment and make some determination of what it says about your communications tool box.

		Yes	No
1.	I find it easy communicating with strangers.	☐	☐
2.	I avoid speaking opportunities.	☐	☐
3.	I am comfortable speaking with persons in authority.	☐	☐
4.	I use words to express myself.	☐	☐
5.	I pronounce all sounds in words accurately.	☐	☐
6.	I speak and make eye contact with my listener.	☐	☐
7.	I get my intended message across immediately.	☐	☐
8.	I communicate well with my spouse or significant other.	☐	☐
9.	I speak at a rate that is neither too fast nor too slow.	☐	☐
10.	I use Standard American English with ease.	☐	☐
11.	I listen and learn from others.	☐	☐

Communication skills can be learned for effective interpersonal exchange. This chapter will provide theory, techniques, exercises and suggestions to aid in achieving ease, confidence and effectiveness in communicating. Put this information into practice for positive communication experiences during your personal and business inter-actions for increased profits, increased self-esteem, increased confidence and vocational success.

"Truth needs no proof...It only needs a witness to it."
—Alfred Stewart, Sr., Ph.D.

What is communication?

Communication is the act of conveying a message that is not linear, but involves a dynamic interaction process between a speaker and listener. Communication is an exchange of information that is shared in a truthful, complete and timely manner in an attempt to reduce ambiguity and uncertainty. Basically, communication is a 'meeting of meaning.' According to Dr. Stephen Covey, "the greatest need of a human being...is to be understood, to be affirmed, to be validated, to be appreciated."

EXERCISE 2: Mental Checklist

The following is a mental checklist for each communication exchange relative to your role as the speaker or listener. Referring to this checklist during each interaction should help you to remain focused on your responsibilities as you strive to achieve understanding.

Speaker's Role:

	Yes	No
1. Do I know what I want to convey?	☐	☐
2. Is my message clear?	☐	☐
3. Is my message ambiguous?	☐	☐
4. Am I using words that are understandable?	☐	☐
5. Are the words arranged grammatically so my message is understood?	☐	☐
6. Am I acknowledging the listener's feedback?	☐	☐
7. Am I modifying my message based upon the listener's feedback?	☐	☐

Listener's Role:

	Yes	No
1. Do I have focused attention on the speaker?	☐	☐
2. Am I making eye contact with the speaker?	☐	☐
3. Am I receiving the speaker's entire message?	☐	☐
4. Am I understanding the speaker's message?	☐	☐
5. Am I open to listening to the speaker's message, sincerely?	☐	☐
6. Am I actively participating by giving genuine feedback to the speaker?	☐	☐

Having this checklist running in the background should help you stay focused and allow you to make, in the moment, corrections necessary for speaking and/or listening effectively.

> *"The reason we have two ears and one mouth is, so that we may listen more and talk less."*
> —*Diogenes*

What is listening?

Listening is a psychological process that involves the act of hearing, as well as gaining information from all of our senses. As an art and a skill, listening is an active process that reflects empathy and the ability to put the other person's needs as a top priority. Consider:

• Are you interested in the topic or person speaking?

• Can you hear the message?

• Is something distracting you?

• Are you tired or sick?

• Are you late for an appointment?

• Do you want to be somewhere else?

Listening is your priority during all communication interactions.

EXERCISE 3: Evaluate Listening Style

Evaluate your listening style and determine the frequency with which you engage in each level. Indicate the circumstance that causes the listening style to emerge, i.e., job, acquaintance, uninteresting topic, friend, lover, spouse, unplanned meeting, or other.

	Never	Sometimes	Always
1. **Ignoring** (I do not pay attention to the other person or what's being said.)	☐	☐	☐
Circumstance: _____			
2. **Pretend** (I acknowledge the other person and act like I am listening; my attention is elsewhere.)	☐	☐	☐
Circumstance: _____			
3. **Selective** (I hear some things and ignore others.)	☐	☐	☐
Circumstance: _____			
4. **Active** (I listen fully, but only to the content.)	☐	☐	☐
Circumstance: _____			
5 **Empathetic** (I listen for the emotion that is present in the message.)	☐	☐	☐
Circumstance: _____			

Of these five levels of listening, the most beneficial for you on the job is active listening, which is "listening with a purpose." This type of listening shows the speaker that he or she is being heard.

EXERCISE 4: Active Listening

Put a check on the line next to the active listening behaviors you practice consistently when you listen. Make a list of those behaviors you did not check for future reference.

___I listen to the speaker.

___I let the speaker finish his sentence or thoughts.

___I give a feedback response after the speaker has finished speaking.

___I give a timely feedback response to prevent unnecessary interruptions.

___I ask open-ended clarifying questions.

___I am open-minded.

___I stay focused on the topic being discussed.

___I paraphrase what the person is saying by stating facts.

___I use positive non-verbal communication by making eye contact, nodding my head, keeping my body position and leaning toward the speaker.

___I demonstrate empathy.

Based on the number of checked responses, your listening behavior score reveals the following:

1–3: Poor listening skills

4–6: Moderately severe listening skills

6–8: Average listening skills

  9: Good listening skills

Perceptions play a role in communication. Often, people's interpretations and inferences become the basis for facts about a person's intentions and attitudes as their own biases, insecurities and prior perceptions confirm these facts. Frequently, office politics result and fester because an apparent established and acceptable practice by managers and supervisors exists. The tone is set from the top. Bickering, complaining, sabotaging, disparate treatment, and discrimination can have a domino effect on the organization's operation if left unchecked or the manager is not skilled in dealing with the conflict.

The following approaches, if practiced, may result in improved relationships:

• Deal with the issue, not the person.

• Actively listen.

• Express emotions constructively.

• Acknowledge feelings of others.

• Have mutual ownership in problem resolution.

• Use "I" phrases and nonverbal behaviors that demonstrate
  direct communication.

• Focus on the needs and interests.

• Recognize conflict as a natural occurrence in the workplace.

Once you have mastered the listening behaviors, you should experience the following benefits:

• Improved customer service.

• More effective communications.

• Increased productivity.

• More effective problem solving.

• Improved conflict management.

What are components of effective communication?

Two basic components that ensure effective communication are *clarity* and *questions*. Clarity relates to one of three types of communication you use.

Assertive Communication is clear, direct, specific, and timely. This is the behavior that allows you to stand up for your rights while at the same time respecting the rights of the other party because you use specific information that reduces the potential for ambiguity or misunderstanding.

Aggressive Communication is explosive, full of emotion and often irrational. This forceful behavior is intended to meet your needs and no one else's. It has a self-serving, brash, loud, and combative behavior and a purpose not intended to help, but to blame. It also tends to beget aggressive behavior.

Non-Assertive Communication is considered passive as minimal remarks or feedback occur initially; responses may be more introspective and internalized. However, over time, it has the potential of being aggressive communication.

At some point, all three types may be appropriate; however, assertive communication is the standard for business and long-standing inter-personal relationships.

The following effective feedback guidelines are useful:

• Deal in specifics.

• Focus on actions, not attitude.

• Determine the appropriate time and place.

• Withhold judgment.

Communication is often unclear and ineffective because of a simple lack of information when you do not bother to get the information you need because you ask no questions at all. Or, you may ask the right questions, but do not listen to the answers well enough to retain the information you need. To seek understanding, questions are needed. Every question should be aimed "at understanding, increasing clarity and decreasing assumptions" according to John Miller, Jr. When you have a conversation where accurate communication is imperative, he suggests using what he calls the "Rule of Two." This rule requires you to check for understanding by asking at least two questions prior to responding to the initial comment.

PURPOSE	QUESTION TYPE	EXAMPLES
Elicit conversation Produce extra thoughts or options	**OPEN**: Questions which allow for a broad range of answers not controlled by the questioner.	"How may I help you?" "What can I do for you?" "How can we work this out?"
Seek additional information	**PROBING**: Short questions that restate the speaker's main points and ask if it is correct.	"So....?" "What else?" "What more could you say about that?" "In what way?" "And....?"
Confirm meaning	**PARAPHRASE**: Questions that restate the content of the speaker's message and ask if it is correct. OR **REFLECT**: Questions which restate the speaker's emotion in the message and seek verification of that emotion.	"Are you saying....?" "If I understand correctly, your main concern is?" "Let me see if I got all the facts right. What happened was....Did I miss anything?" My sense is that you're feeling...Am I correct?" "You sound (look)...; Am I close?" "So, you're really...?"
Offer explanations	**OPEN**	"What if I/we...?" "What might happen if we did?" "What about...?"

The previous chart reveals question types according to intent that focus on communicating to understand.

How important is nonverbal communication?

Have you had a conversation with someone who reported information based on what another person said? If so, possibly what you heard was a partial picture of the actual story. Information is gained from body posture, gestures, facial expressions, eye contact, and proxemics (use of space). Sometimes this information may amplify or contradict the actual words you speak. The bulk of your message comes from nonverbal behaviors. Your ability to interpret mixed messages, unclear messages and implied messages will give you a jump start in implementing the techniques to ensure a meeting of meanings and a sharing of information.

What does your voice say about you?
EXERCISE 5: Emphasis

Read the sentences below by stressing <u>the underlined word </u>in each sentence. Notice how the meaning of the sentence changes as you emphasize a different word in the same sentence. Then, ask a friend or colleague to interpret the meaning of each sentence that you read. Do the interpretations match your intention?

"I didn't tell her you were sick."

"<u>I</u> didn't tell her you were sick."
(Somebody else told her.)

"I <u>didn't</u> tell her you were sick."
(I emphatically did not.)

"I didn't <u>tell</u> her you were sick."
(I implied it)

"I didn't tell <u>her</u> you were sick."
(I told someone else.)

"I didn't tell her <u>you</u> were sick."
(I told her someone else was sick.)

"I didn't tell her you <u>were</u> sick."
(I told her you're still sick.) '

"I didn't tell her you were <u>sick</u>."
(I told her something else about you.)

> *"Small minds discuss people. Average minds discuss events.*
> *Great minds discuss ideas."*
> *—Anonymous*

Is this walking on eggshells?

Sometimes words are not selected, but blurted without careful consideration. Saying the first thought that comes to mind may be more problematic and seem impulsively harsh, demanding, insensitive, uncaring or rude. Responses do not have to be given in a split-second. Pause time can be meaningful and beneficial. The words you choose may leave a lasting impression about your personality, as well as your communication skills. Practice saying a considerate phrase when someone asks a question or makes a statement that may cause you to give a defensive response. Refer to the list below for examples:

Considerate Responses
• "I can…"
• "It would help if you…"
• "Here are some options…Consider these alternatives…"
• "Let me clarify…"
• "The best way I can help is…" "Let me see what I can do…"
• "My understanding is…"
• "I'll find out…" "Let me get someone who can…"
• "I know who can help… "

How does self-disclosure impact communication?

The amount of information an individual chooses to disclose is going to depend on the situation and relationship. Some information may not be disclosed because it may not have importance to the business or personal relationship. However, honest and open communications provide the foundation for a healthy work environment. In this type of environment, you feel free to express yourself openly. You feel you are being heard and that your contribution adds value to the organization. This willingness to self-disclose can eventually "lead to a greater level of trust, honest participation and learningful dialogue," according to John Miller, Jr.

EXERCISE 6: Needs Assessment

By now you are aware of your communication style. Complete the survey about your needs regarding your communication skills.

	Yes	No
1. I need to improve my ability to communicate with strangers.	☐	☐
2. I need to accept speaking opportunities.	☐	☐
3. I need to be comfortable speaking with persons in authority.	☐	☐
4. I need to use words accurately.	☐	☐
5. I need to improve my pronunciation skills.	☐	☐
6. I need to be comfortable making eye contact when I speak.	☐	☐
7. I need to get my intended message across immediately.	☐	☐
8. I need to improve how I communicate with my spouse or significant other.	☐	☐
9. I need to learn how to speak at a rate that is neither too fast nor too slow.	☐	☐
10. I need to use Standard American English with ease.	☐	☐
11. I need to improve my listening skills so I can learn from others.	☐	☐

EXERCISE 7: Improvement Plan

Review the areas you indicated need improvement and list each on a separate sheet of paper. Decide which one behavior you want to start improving and how you will measure your progress. Next, identify the barriers you think you will encounter and write down specific actions you will take to reduce or eliminate each barrier in order to reach your goal. Devote one week to your action plan, allowing for at least 10 minutes a day towards strengthening that particular skill. Track and record your daily progress. At the end of one week, re-assess your progress and determine if you feel comfortable enough to address a new behavior from the list. Refer to some of the suggestions in this chapter as a guide.

Example:

Problem: History of conflict with a certain staff member and the usual response is ignoring or using thoughtless words.

Goal: Use thoughtful words during feedback.

Barriers: Tend to be impulsive and reactive. Difficulty inhibiting gut reactions.

Action Plan: Use the "Rule of Two" by asking at least two questions.

Communication is inevitable and the benefits can be enormous when the emphasis is on implementing the skills needed to achieve mutual understanding. When the process involves truth, sincerity and judicious disclosure while employing effective speaking and listening skills, your path to varied communication encounters will lead to personal satisfaction and success.

Good luck on your path to many rewarding communication experiences.

ABOUT THE AUTHOR

MARY PAUL

Mary Paul is the Senior Organization Development and Training Manager for Harley-Davidson Motor Company's Powertrain Operations and Juneau Avenue Corporate Headquarters in Milwaukee Wisconsin. Mary's primary responsibilities include taking a leadership role in the design and development of organizational change efforts that are consistent with evolving organizational needs and business requirements. She also assists in the development of strategies for and provides coaching to Harley-Davidson Leadership to identify training needs and create appropriate actions to meet those needs to support the organization's strategic plan.

Prior to her current role, Mary has held several positions within Harley-Davidson, including being a Program Manager for Rider's Edge Motorcycle Training program, plus various positions within the Organization Development and Training Department.

In the past, Mary has also held management positions with Anheuser-Busch Companies and Sara Lee in St. Louis, Missouri.

Committed to her profession, Mary is also a member of a number of professional business organizations including The Professional Woman Network, Professional Dimensions, Women in Networking, and the American Society for Training and Development.

Contact:
Organization Development and Training Manager
Harley-Davidson Motor Company
5801 S. Oak Road
West Bend, WI 53095
(414) 343-7340
mary.paul@harley-davidson.com

EIGHTEEN

TRANSITIONING INTO MANAGEMENT

By Mary Paul

Being a manager is one of the most rewarding aspects of becoming a professional woman. This chapter is dedicated to helping you reap the rewards of being a successful manager, which will benefit you not only as a new manager, but will also last well into your career.

More and more organizations are actively looking for women to join their management ranks. There are two important reasons to hire, promote, and retain talented women: demographic changes due to a continuously dropping birth rate and the growing need for diversity. Furthermore, women are being called the new managers for the 21st century. (Vickenburg, Jansen, and Koopman, *Women in Management*, London, Sage Publications, 2000.)

As organizations move from a more hierarchical structure with a traditional leadership style to one of empowered work-teams calling for high involvement, the preferred leadership style is being described in more feminine terms such as building alliances and developing others. In Marcus Buckingham's and Curt Coffman's book, *First, Break All The*

Rules, the authors' main point is to first take stock of your employees' strengths, then build upon those strengths to create a phenomenal workforce. This method obviously makes sense, but is not the usual method used by most managers today. Many managers still focus on their employees' weaknesses, thus never taking advantage of an employee's strengths, thereby eventually de-motivating their staff. There's an old management adage: you are only as good as your team is. Therefore, the first place to start if you want to move into management is with *you*.

This chapter is divided into three sections: Preparing for a Management Role, Transitioning into a Management Role, and Tips for being Successful as a New Manager.

Preparing For a Management Role:

So, you've been thinking you're ready to take on greater responsibility in your job, and you've been thinking about a management role. Being in a management position can mean several different roles. You can be a front-line supervisor with direct reports responsible for a particular function of a business, or a project manager with responsibility for a project and supervising a team of people assigned to the project for a period of time, or an entrepreneur where you have decided to manage your own business.

Regardless of which type of management you choose to go into, preparation is the key. The more time you spend doing your homework and preparing yourself for your new management role, the more successful you will become. Believe me, not many women who are successful managers "just fell into it naturally." They spent their fair share of time preparing to be successful by considering the items that follow, and seeing what fit best for them.

- **Identify your goals.** Take stock of your current situation and what type of management you want to move towards. In addition, consider your timeline, when do you aspire to be in your first management role? You cannot always control the clock, but you can use time as a gauge to see if you are moving toward your goals.

- **Assess your strengths and areas for development.** There are many assessments available online, through career counselors and Human Resources departments which can assist you in identifying your leadership style, and areas of strength and areas for development. Some common assessments are the "Leadership Styles" assessment from Human Synergistics at www.humansynergistics.com, and the Myer's-Briggs Type Indicator (MBTI), though not primarily used for leadership assessment, has many books and articles written for each type that can provide powerful insight into the style of leader you may be based on your MBTI type.

- **Check within your own company.** See if there is a Career Development or Employee Development department, or someone (usually within Human Resources or Training) with that specialty. These in-house professionals can be very helpful by providing leadership assessments, defined competencies that may exist in your organization for employees, and job specifications for managers. They can also assist you in creating a robust development plan with creative ideas and education designed to move you into a management position.

- Your company may also have a **competency-based 360-degree assessment process,** whereby you can solicit input from your current supervisor, peers, and stakeholders on identified competencies for your current role. This 360-degree assessment gives you valuable information because it generates feedback from multiple levels of people who interact with you, (hence the name 360-degree). 360-degree assessments are commonly used by Human Resource functions such as Training and Organization Development. Check with the professionals in those areas for more information.

- Another item to investigate is the **educational level** required for managers within your company. Many companies insist on a Bachelor's degree to be in a management role, regardless of the amount of real-life experience you may have. Don't be discouraged, even if your company requires a degree, and you don't have one. Often just registering and beginning to work toward your degree, along with your work experience is enough to open the managerial door for you.

- **Watch the postings board** at your company to see what the requirements are for management roles. Requirements will vary depending upon the responsibility level of the position, but take note of not only the credentials required, but also the leadership responsibilities and the behaviors required. These are often in the body of the job posting, for example: "Has primary responsibility for consulting with key leaders as they initiate and manage change within their departments/groups in support of business objectives." This line reveals that the manager must have change management process and coaching skills, as well as be able to influence and build alliances with upper management.

- **Network, network, network.** You've heard this before, but networking is the most important thing you can do as you seek to move into a management role. Networking for career development is only beginning to gain importance among women in the past few years. There are both informal and formal networks available to women. Informal networks are relationships formed by choice with a like goal, task, or social need in mind. Formal networks involve a specified group of people who form relationships and meet periodically providing mutual benefit by building alliances and sharing information among their members.

There are many types of formal networks available to you. Check the local business section of the daily newspaper identifying business networks that exist in your community. In addition, check the Internet to see what types of networks are available for your occupational interest. There are many women's networks dedicated to the development of women of all ages. Many of these networks meet on a monthly basis over a meal to share job information, social interaction, and many have programs with speakers targeted on women's development issues. Check out www.quintcareers.com for an up-to-date listing of women's networking organizations.

In addition, many companies have internal networks for women that are formed to share similar concerns among women employees. Ask your Human Resources representative if any of these internal networks for women exist.

• Check to see if your company or networking organization has a **formal mentoring program**. Mentoring is based on the needs of the individual requesting such a relationship. Discussions focus on the future, and can include topics such as education, career aspirations, known strengths, and personal interests, as well as developmental opportunities. These are designed to improve rapport, open communication, and create meaningful partnerships.

Even if your organization does not have a formal mentoring program, you may choose to approach a manager you admire to be an informal mentor. Do your homework before approaching a possible mentor, by clarifying your interests, values, strengths, and developmental opportunities, identifying long-term goals, and some developmental activities. Finally, create your agenda for the first development discussion by focusing on assessing your current strengths and areas for development. Another great place to look for mentoring in specific career fields is by doing a search on the Internet. Many mentoring organizations are listed by their field of specialty.

One key to moving into a management position is visibility. One way to increase your visibility and share your interest for moving into a management position is to set up some informational interviews with managers in your organization. An informational interview is an appointment that you schedule with a particular individual for the purpose of gaining information from an "insider's" point of view to explore your possibilities. Unlike job interviews, information interviews do not require that you sell yourself and do not depend on existing job vacancies. Informational interviews are arranged with those likely to provide information directly or with those who can refer you to persons with the information you are seeking. You will also want to select individuals who are managers in areas you have an interest in. Even if you don't know them, most people will be happy to spend 30-minutes talking about their jobs. Just make sure you are very clear in letting them know the purpose for the meeting is for information only, and you are not looking for a particular job; this helps relieve any sense of obligation on the part of the person you are interviewing.

Start the interview stating that you want to learn about what the individual is responsible for, what skills and competencies are necessary for success and development, ideas in order to help you prepare for a management role. Keep the conversation casual, ask questions for clarity and thank the individual for his or her time. Be sure to send a thank-you note after your meeting; you never know when a job opening may come up in that area and the manager you interviewed remembers you were interested in working in the area.

Another way to gain management experience is by requesting challenging assignments and projects that improve your leadership skills. These do not have to be projects or assignments just at work. These assignments could be in your current area at work, on work-related task-forces or committees, or in community or professional organizations. Look for assignments where you can either be the team leader or share in leadership responsibilities. Working on assignments and projects such as these demonstrates that you are willing to go above and beyond your regular duties, take on new challenges and increase your visibility to additional managers in your organization.

Transitioning into a Management Role:
Alright, you've landed a management position! You're excited and want to do your very best, but what should you pay attention to during that all-important transition period? (The period from when you accept the new management role through your first couple of weeks on the job.) This is a critical time for you; your transition period into a management role sets the tone for how quickly you will become a fully contributing leader in your organization. In addition, a successful transition can help you feel more connected to your new role and the people you will be working with.

This is a very challenging time for a new manager with two separate paths, intellectual and emotional. Most new manager transition (sometimes called assimilation) processes, if you are lucky enough to have one where you work, only focus on the intellectual path, what you need to know as a new manager: budgets, payroll, goal-setting, product knowledge, scheduling, disciplinary procedures, etc. However, the emotional path can have many ups and downs for the new manager, such as:

• Are you now supervising former peers?

• Did any of your new direct reports also apply for your new position?

• Have you worked with any of your new management-level peers before?

• Are you being transferred to a new division or department?

• If you are in a new department, do you know anyone, supervisor, peers or direct reports?

• If you are in a new department, how familiar are you with their processes?

• What about arranging for setup of your desk, phone, computer, moving your files? (Don't laugh; this can often be very frustrating!)

• Did anyone tell the new staff you were coming? What was said about you?

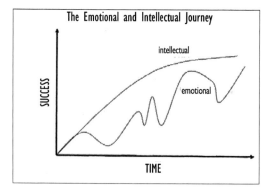

Downey, Diane: Assimilating New Leaders, New York, ANACOM, 2001.

These situations (plus countless more) can cause considerable anxiety on the part of a new manager. You want to make the best impression and not appear pushy, yet how do you determine that the previous situations have been taken care of, and if they have not, how do you go about taking care of them yourself?

The first thing to do is check with your Human Resources representative to see if your company has a transition process. If so, work closely with your Human Resources representative and hiring manager to involve yourself in the process. If your company does not have a transition process, you can create your own with a little help from Human Resources and your new hiring manager.

The three basic components of assuring a successful transition into a management position are planning, entering, and follow-through.

Planning:

• The hiring manager verifies when he/she will be announcing your promotion to staff members.

• In addition, the hiring manager should inform key stakeholders about your promotion. Key stakeholders include individuals and groups with whom you will have close contact, such as external suppliers, internal teams and management groups.

• Finally, identify who will be helping you with administrative setup. This can often be one of the most frustrating transition spots for a new manager. Just getting settled into your new workspace properly can make a big difference in your ability to quickly transition to your new role.

Here is a basic administrative checklist for your use:

Administrative Checklist

- Office Space
- Desk
- Chair
- Computer
- Special Software Access
- Printer Connection
- Fax Connection
- Phone/Voicemail
- Employee Directory
- Business Cards
- Cell phone/pager
- Mailroom and receptionist notified
- Personal Digital Assistant (e.g. Palm Pilot/IPAC)
- Reference materials (e.g. department strategies, product catalogs, organization charts, etc.)

Entering:

Set up brief (30 minute) introductory meetings with the following individuals or groups:

- **Hiring Manager**: Topics for this meeting include performance expectations, priorities, and current projects.

- **Direct Reports/Project Team Members**: Meet individually with each of your direct reports. Meeting individually with each of your direct reports gives the two of you a chance for some one-on-one time to discuss current assignments, performance standards, interpersonal style/communication preferences, and their career goals. If you are managing a project team, hold an introductory team meeting with all members to update you on the project status, while you and each team member share information regarding background, team role, and interpersonal style/communication preferences. This introductory meeting with a project team helps to get the team on a more comfortable level for working with you as their new team manager.

- **Key Stakeholders**: Schedule a short meeting with individuals and groups you will be working with as a new manager. You may also choose to reserve 30 minutes of an already-scheduled meeting for you to cover the following: introductions, your background, primary role and responsibilities. In addition, ask your key stakeholders questions regarding priorities, upcoming challenges or issues you need to be aware of.

Follow-through:

• Schedule bi-monthly "follow-up" meetings with your hiring manager, and direct reports or team members, to keep abreast of changing priorities, challenges, and career development. Regular communication in the early stages of your managerial transition keeps everyone "on the same page," and avoids surprises helping to ease some of the emotional angst you experience as a new manager.

• In addition to "follow-up" meetings with those mentioned previously, keep up with your networking skills. Periodically, meet informally with your key stakeholders, perhaps over a cup of coffee, to assure their needs and expectations are being met. These actions also keep you visible with your key stakeholders in more than just a formal setting and can build alliances for future projects.

Tips for Being a Successful New Manager:

Being a new manager is an exciting time, you now have both the responsibility and the authority to meet the expectations your organization has set out for you and your team. I've been in management for over twenty years, and the best advice anyone ever gave me was to "just be my authentic self." Sometimes new managers can get into trouble with their direct reports or team members when they forget the behaviors and skills which got them selected for the job (like adaptability and coaching), and exhibit behaviors that are controlling and over-directing. Ninety-nine percent of your direct reports or team members will give you one-hundred percent effort if you show them respect and work to provide them with the necessary support and resources to accomplish the task. Take a look at what you want from your manager and strive to meet those same standards.

I wish you well in your management quest; it can be one of the most gratifying aspects of your entire career, whether it leads to a management position or not. But if it does, I hope you will find these tips helpful.

Notes:

_____

_____

_____

_____

_____

_____

_____

_____

_____

_____

_____

_____

_____

_____

_____

_____

_____

_____

_____

_____

ABOUT THE AUTHOR

SHARYN YONKMAN

Sharyn Lynn Yonkman is the founder and principal consultant for Lynn Consulting Group, a personal and professional development training organization. Lynn Consulting specializes in career advancement skills for the professional woman, helping her in achieving personal excellence. As a passionate advocate of women's self-empowerment and life balance issues, Sharyn offers special expertise in dealing with transition and change in the workplace, as well as programs designed for those of the baby-boomer generation.

As former CFO of several high-profile retail and hospitality companies, Ms. Yonkman has gained valuable in-depth financial and managerial experience in the corporate community providing the knowledge for cost-effective solutions for today's business challenges. A sampling of the training programs available includes: Sensitivity and Diversity, Professional Image, Power of the Positive, Professional Customer Service, Self-empowerment, Assertiveness, Handling Conflict and Emotions, Women-Wellness Work, and Getting Over Getting Older. Additionally, customized curriculum is available to meet your specific business needs. One-on-one individual executive personal coaching is also available.

Born, raised, and educated in New Jersey, Sharyn moved to southern California a decade ago. This bi-coastal experience provides her a unique perspective to be able to incorporate the best of each coast's business culture and convey that knowledge to her clients.

Ms. Yonkman is a co-author of *Remarkable Women*, an anthology project with Jennifer O'Neil, Dottie Walters, and Marci Shimoff. Additionally, she is currently completing an upcoming solo project for baby-boomer women facing the challenges of moving from the first act of life to the second. Trainer, motivational speaker, author, and coach, Ms. Yonkman is available internationally to help the individual or organization with professional developmental needs.

Contact:
Lynn Consulting Group
P.O. Box 1266
Ventura, CA 93002
(805) 677-3117
Lynnconsult@yahoo.net
www.protrain.net

NINETEEN

OVERCOMING FEAR

By Sharyn Yonkman

What would you say is the main reason why talented women fall short of their professional goals? You might be surprised to learn that the reason is *fear*. Fear is the roadblock that can keep you from realizing your full potential in life.

In this chapter you will learn techniques and tools to help you name your fears and navigate through your personal roadblocks to success. Let's begin the journey to live your life by decision and not by default.

Fear is Not the problem

Wait a minute. Didn't you just say that fear was the major roadblock keeping women from success? Yes, fear is the roadblock, but not the problem. Our worst fears can turn out to be our best teachers.

In fact, it is how we *deal with* our fear that is the problem. It is vital that we deal with our fears with a sense of power, not pain.

Fear is within us; it is not an external force. Life can be organized chaos and being able to navigate around it successfully takes skill. Much like stress, fears can be either healthy or unhealthy.

Healthy Fears:

• Are real, addressable dangers

• Offer protection and/or guidance

• Inspire us to do what can be done in the present

Unhealthy Fears:

• Are exaggerated and invented dangers

• Require the need to be in control endlessly

• May lead to neurotic behaviors

Like stress, you cannot escape from fear, but you can transform it into a vehicle that will drive you to exciting destinations.

EXERCISE

In the spaces below, list current fears that relate to obtaining your professional goals. Then list some ideas on how you might be able to overcome these fears.

You may want to revisit this list once you have finished reading this chapter.

List your fears	What you will do to overcome them
1. _____	1. _____
2. _____	2. _____
3. _____	3._____
4. _____	4. _____
5. _____	5. _____
6. _____	6. _____
7. _____	7. _____
8. _____	8. _____

Fears are Just Thoughts

What we must remember is that fear is a thought and a thought can be changed. When you change the way you deal with your fears, they lose their power over you. Fearful thoughts will lead to fearful experiences. When you learn to look at your fear in a new light, you can forever alter your perception of fear. This change in your inherent view of fear means you are no longer the captive of its negative stronghold.

Most (almost 90%) of what we dread and worry about never happens. Unhealthy fears are not facts. They are faulty perceptions, a type of mental error that sets up a cycle of fear. This cycle is very similar to our body's reaction to stress, which is the stimulus for the fight-or-flight response. Although this cycle can be very powerful (fear-fight-flight), please know that it can be broken. We can transform this cycle for we have the power to control our thoughts. It is within your power to create a safe world for yourself by changing your thoughts from those of fear to those of safety.

Breathe through your fears. Allow yourself to feel and accept them and then breathe into them with deep belly breathing. Our breathing quickens and becomes shallow when we are fearful which creates stress and anxiety. Relax by switching to deep breathing. Use this relaxation technique anytime or anywhere fear strikes.

BELLY BREATHING EXERCISE

It is vital that you get oxygen to the brain as quickly as possible; therefore, this exercise requires breathing in through the nose and exhaling through the mouth.

•Take a long, deep breath in through your nose and imagine your
 belly inflating like a balloon.

- Exhale through mouth slowly, and completely while visualizing deflating a balloon.

- Repeat.

- This time, on the exhale, blow out slowly and completely but pause and hold for a beat at the bottom of the breath. Enjoy—this is where stillness is. Lovely, quiet, peaceful stillness.

This is a great technique to use to facilitate your meditation or visualization practices.

Consequences of Fear:

- Agitation
- Anxiety
- Dread
- Judgment
- Negativity
- Panic
- Perfectionism
- Procrastination
- Self-consciousness
- Worry

EXERCISE

Take some time to consider in what ways fear may be hampering your progress toward your goals. Then, try to imagine that those fears no longer existed.

This exercise may be used periodically as you work through and identify your roadblocks.

What does living without any fear mean to my career?

_____

_____

_____

If I were fearless, what would I try today?

_____

_____

_____

Do not seek to be protected from danger, but rather strive to be fearless when you face danger.

Fear and Anger

Anger can mask fear. It can be a defense against anxiety and fear. Anger is about unfulfilled desires and unhealthy fear prevents you from meeting your desires.

To prevent anxiety from building up, pay close attention to the messages that your body sends you throughout your busy day. Notice points of tension that may arise. Stretch out or go for a walk to relieve this built-up tension before you allow it to become pain.

Other helpful hints to reduce anxiety:

• Get enough sleep

• Eat healthy foods

• Limit or remove caffeine, alcohol, and sugar

• Increase water intake

• Meditate

• Use relaxation/sleep tapes

Things to avoid:	Things to incorporate:
Blame (yourself or others)	Owning your actions
Playing the victim	Taking responsibility
Negative tapes	Positive self-talk
Rewards that keep you trapped	Future rewards focus

Fear As A Source of Energy and Power

Fear will be in charge as long as you let it, but you can harness the energy of fear that is within you and redirect it. To do so, you must take the fear energy and drive it to power you toward success. Always move toward your fears, for they will only gain strength if you retreat from them. Once you face your fears and take some risks, it will help to energize you to move forward.

Whatever it is you are dreading (i.e., asking for that well-deserved raise) is exactly what you must face. You must do what you fear to help conquer fear. The way to overcome fear is simply by doing the thing you fear. Each step you take makes you stronger.

Remember that everyone experiences fear when he or she attempts something new. We don't have to overcome our fears to enter into this unfamiliar territory; we just have to show up there. Showing up has power and breeds courage, which is contagious. There is great power and energy generated by taking action.

Pushing through fear is less frightening than living with the feeling of helplessness or the dread that accompanies it. When you choose a path of growth and action, it is most powerful. It reminds us that we do have choices and that there is great power within ourselves and our ability to choose.

Fear robs us of time by taking our attention from our creativity and our ability to solve problems and instead only focuses our attentions on the perceived danger confronting us.

Worrying is not planning! Do not mistake one for the other.

Planning	Results	Worrying	Results
Has purpose	Positive changes	Non-constructive	Confusion
Goal-oriented	Increased energy	Powered by fear	Exhaustion

Reframe your thoughts and shift your gears from worrying to planning.

EXERCISE
Your subconscious believes what it hears, not what is! So make sure it only "hears" a powerful, fearless vocabulary. Start paying close attention to your speech, as well as to your thought patterns, to note when you are speaking from a place of powerlessness and reframe your speech and thoughts to those of power, as in the examples below.

Try this Powerful Vocabulary
1. Instead of......"I hope", say......"I know."
2. Instead of......"I can't", say......"I won't."
3. Instead of.... ..."If only", say......"Next time."

In the following spaces, list some of your current powerless communications and then reframe them to the more powerful model.

1."I hope"

_____

Reframe
"I know"_____

2. "I can't" _____
Reframe
"I won't" _____

3. "If only"_____

   Reframe

   "Next time"_____

Fear of Failure

Fear of failure is due to a lack of self-confidence. You must replace uncertainty with confidence in yourself to overcome your fear of failure. This process may require you to work on self-esteem issues to produce the confidence it takes to overcome fear.

Fear of making a mistake is a waste of your valuable time. Instead of fearing mistakes, you should be more fearful of not making any mistakes. If you are not making any mistakes, it most likely means that you are not trying hard enough to grow.

Self-confidence is critical to enable you to decide that you can deal with your fears and take risks. Willingness to take risks is a mindset of success and fear is your roadblock. You can say that you are not a risktaker, but then you must be prepared to leave the rewards to those who dare to risk. You have the courage and the power to take risks and succeed, so don't be the one left behind for fear of taking risks.

If fear and the desire to reach your goals collide, which one will prevail?

Be sure to keep in mind that if you do happen to fail it does not make you a failure. It only means that you failed at that particular task. You are not your behavior and you certainly are not a failure. Adversity does not have to triumph over you, for you can cope with outcomes that are less than perfect.

Do not engage in over-generalization. Things do not have to be perceived as all or nothing

Historically, women have had a special relationship with fear because they were told not to take risks; they were told to be careful. Not taking risks is a product of our learned culture and instills fear.

The exercise below is a tool to help you develop your tolerance of risk-taking.

EXERCISE

In order to build your self confidence, you must be willing to take risks so that you can prove to yourself that you are more than capable of reaching your goals. The risks do not have to be monumental to accomplish this goal, just something that makes you uncomfortable. Each day take a risk of the type that helps to build your sense of self-worth. Your fears did not appear overnight, nor will they disappear that quickly. Reprogramming habits takes time and work. It takes at least three weeks to instill new habits, so you must be patient and persistent.

Risk I am willing to take   **Outcome**

Week #1

Monday_____   _____

Tuesday_____   _____

Wednesday_____   _____

Thursday_____   _____

Friday_____   _____

Be my guest, take the weekends off.

Risk I am willing to take   Outcome

Week #2

Monday_____   _____

Tuesday_____   _____

Wednesday_____   _____

Thursday_____   _____

Friday_____   _____

Week #3

Monday_____   _____

Tuesday_____   _____

Wednesday_____

Thursday_____   _____

Friday_____

Chart your progress for the next three weeks.

Fear of Success

Just as paralyzing as the fear of failure is the fear of success. Yes, that's right, the fear of success! You might ask why talented women would fear becoming successful.

Unfortunately, success for women goes against some long-held cultural stereotypes. It breaks the old rules. It may lead to the fear of exclusion and rejection and penalize successful women for breaking those outdated social rules. These stereotypes have evolved some in recent years, but we all know we still have a way to go. The challenge for today's successful professional woman is to protect her beliefs about her ability to succeed while breaking those obsolete rules.

Fear of self-acknowledgment is a type of fear of success you might never have thought of, but it does exist. It is the fear of realizing you really are competent and capable of greatness. Imagine that! Being successful would make this a fact. If your self-image isn't up to success, this change in perception of your worth might seem too extreme. With success comes increased responsibilities and greater expectations from others. This may lead to perfectionism, rigidity, or withdrawal, but certainly does not have to. You are in control of your attitude and you should remember that true success is always personally defined.

Keep Your Fears From Blocking Your Progress
• Experiment
• Acknowledge true feelings
• Address negative self talk
• Learn to let go
• Break things down into small steps
• Nurture yourself
• Practice daily

EXERCISE
This exercise is a call for action from you to learn to overcome the fear of success. First, list reasons and/or explanations of why you have not yet reached your goals completely or realized the fullest extent of your ability and talents. Attach to these reasons/explanations the type of fear that is responsible. Then note ways to eliminate each of the fears.

Reason	Fear	Remove
_____	_____	_____
_____	_____	_____
_____	_____	_____

Managing Your Fear to Manage Your Career

Fear can become a bad habit and one you cannot afford to indulge in if you are to achieve your professional goals. When allowed to take control, fear can kill careers, dreams, and hopes by igniting self-sabotage. Develop your trust in yourself and the fear will be manageable.

Fears that keep women from challenging others in the workplace

Decision-making is another area in your professional life where fear may derail you from the fast track to success. The fear associated with making the "wrong" decision can keep you from making any decision. Merely by not choosing, you are choosing. You are choosing to do nothing and to deprive yourself of any new experiences and growth that you might have enjoyed.

The key to fearless decision-making, as in so many things in your professional life, is to do your homework. Information and knowledge are power and will help lead you to your best possible choice. Armed with sufficient information, establish your priorities (not those of others) and focus on the fact that trusting your instinct is key. This will help you to arrive at an informed and insightful decision, without letting fear immobilize you by always trying to foresee the future.

After making your decision, let go of your expectations and do not create unnecessary angst by trying to control the outcome of your decision. Instead, adopt a "Can't Lose" policy about the outcome by looking forward to the opportunity for learning and growing even if things do not work out. If things do not turn out as anticipated, you can always change your course and adjust your actions to secure success. This is truly "no losing–no fear" decision making in action.

To Summarize:

• Develop strong self-esteem.

• Practice positive self-talk.

• Gain knowledge.

• Establish your priorities.

• Trust your gut instincts.

• Let go.

• Learn from missteps.

• Adjust actions if necessary.

EXERCISE

Think about something in your professional life that you need to make a decision about and in the following spaces write down both options. Think about what fears are associated with each of these choices and fill those in. Now, focus on the positives for each scenario and list all the pluses for each. You will note that this is not the typical pros/cons approach to decision-making. It is a focus on the positive spin. It is "no lose decision-making"

For example, you must decide on making a lateral move to a division of your company that is closer to your home. Obviously, your choices are *stay* or *move*. What fears materialize when you think of both situations? Stay–*Loss of possibilities*, Move–*Uncertainty*. What pluses are there for each path available? Stay–*comfortable with environment, like the people*. Move–*closer to home, save commuting time and costs*.

The purpose of this exercise is for you to learn to focus on "no lose," therefore, insuring whatever decision you make has value. Either way you win. You have nothing to lose except your fear.

Choice A	Fear	Pluses+
_____	_____	_____
_____	_____	_____
_____	_____	_____

Choice B	Fears	Pluses+
_____	_____	_____
_____	_____	_____
_____	_____	_____

I hope you have acquired some useful tips from this chapter and will find them helpful in navigating around your fearful roadblocks. Enjoy your journey to fearlessness. Buckle up, buckle down, and full speed ahead.

Resources
Feel the Fear and Do It Anyway by Susan Jeffers, Fawcett Columbine, New York, NY (1987).

How to Control Your Anxiety Before It Controls You, by Albert Ellis, Ph.D., Birch Lane Press (1998).

Embracing Fear & Finding the Courage to Live Your Life, by Thomas Rutledge, Harper Collins, New York, NY (2002).

Fearless Living by Rhonda Britten, Perigree Books (2002).

Notes:

ABOUT THE AUTHOR

DIANE CAIN

Diane Cain is the founder and President of The Focus Group, an organization development, professional development, and training consulting service. Her past work experiences as a non-profit executive director, a sixteen-year corporate director, and as adjunct faculty for a community college, have prepared her to offer consulting services on a broad spectrum of subjects.

She is known and respected as a dynamic professional with a unique blend of knowledge and skills. She is an accomplished leader, educator, trainer, mentor, coach, and motivational speaker.

She has researched, developed, and facilitated seminars on a wide range of topics with an emphasis on diversity, beyond race and gender, as a business driver in today's workplace. She has provided consultation to Fortune 100 corporations, not-for-profit organizations, colleges, urban school organizations, quick-service, and dine-in restaurant establishments.

Diane's academic credentials include a BS with distinction in Organization Management and an MA in Organization Development. She is a certified in Youth Development, Diversity Facilitation, International Human Resource Management and additional areas of expertise.

Diane is a member and leader of many professional organizations including: Gary (IN) Business and Professional Women, International Board of Advisors of The Professional Woman Network (Louisville, Kentucky), International Advisory Board of Red Cross of Northwest Indiana, and the National Association of Female Executives.

Contact
The Focus Group
dicain@peoplepc.com
www.protrain.net

TWENTY

UNDERSTANDING DIVERSITY

By Diane Cain

Many of you are tempted at this point not to read this section of the book. You have had similar discussions in the past, and possibly some heated arguments with friends and family on the subject. You were possibly required to attend a class in college or high school that also covered the subject. Now, here it is again—DIVERSITY—in print. However, please find a comfy chair and continue your journey in self-development.

This section is written with one objective: to engage your whole brain in the understanding of diversity. Research tells us that the left brain is analytical and logical; the right brain is intuitive and holistic. As you explore the broad subject of diversity, you may find yourself extracting energies from both sides.

Here is my promise to you—gems of wisdom and carats of self-realization await you in the coming pages as you seek to understand the importance and impact of diversity. Enjoy!

Each person's map of the world is as unique as the person's thumbprint.
There are no two people alike.
No two people who understand the same sentence the same way.
So in dealing with people, you try not to fit them to your
concept of what they should be.
—*Milton Erickson*

The term "diversity" refers to differences. There are many labels attached to the word diversity, for example: race, gender, ethnicity, cultural background, age, sexual orientation, religion, physical ability, and mental capability. It also refers to the many ways we are different in other respects: work style, personality, class, education, marital status, demographics, problem-solving approaches, communication styles, and life experiences. However, how does it apply to you and to your professional development journey?

Ask yourself the following questions. Jot down your responses after giving thoughtful, truthful answers to each one. Caution: there is no right or wrong answer, just your answer based on your personal perspectives.

What is your comfort level with those that do not look like you? Circle the most appropriate number on the grid:

(very comfortable) 1-----2-----3----4-----5 (very uncomfortable)

Is there a particular difference that makes you uncomfortable? Please name it:

_____

_____

Have you ever been the victim of discrimination or stereotypical thinking?

___ Yes ___ No If yes, what impact does the experience currently carry in
                your life?

_____

_____

Are you ethnocentric? _____ Yes _____ No
Why did you give that answer?

_____

_____

What is your adaptability to change threshold?

Circle one of the answers below:

• I am a quick change artist.

• It takes me a while to study all the indicators and data.

• I prefer the "good old days."

Diversity is a complex subject. However, be mindful that few diversity
conflicts are race-neutral or gender-neutral. Let's pretend for a moment
that you are privy to the following scenario:

> *A man and a woman are driving cross country in their luxury*
> *sedan. The man is in the driver's seat. He is not listening to the*
> *woman's urging that they made a wrong turn about ten miles back.*
> *He is thinking: "Why doesn't she stop that nagging! I know where I am*
> *going." She is thinking, he's a man, he won't listen to common sense.*
> *At the root of the scenario, their gender has little to do with the problem.*

Reflect on your answers to the previous questions for a minute.
However, please withhold judging yourself. Conscious self-probing
about the way you handle diverse interactions will reap self-discovery
benefits for your professional development. These carats of self-

realization are a sampling of the ingredients that make you a unique, diverse individual. You are on the threshold of a world of opportunities.

You may be beginning a new career or re-thinking your current career. Regardless of where you are today, you are participating in a most dynamic environment. Leaders realize that demographic, global, and technology shifts are pushing critical issues to the surface. One of those critical issues surrounds the subsequent conflicts caused by differences.

Story Time

Once upon a time there was a consultant that facilitated a class on leveraging diversity at a client's office. The class participants desired to talk about gender styles and cross-cultural communications. These were perceived as areas of difficulty within the organization. It was a robust exchange.

The majority of the participants were under the age of 35 and college-educated. They desired a logical, systematic approach to 'new' diversity learning. They all agreed that they had been through this before. They needed something tangible to take back to their offices. They needed tools that could be immediately used.

After much discussion, consensus was reached on four helpful rules (tools):

• *Assume differences until similarity is proven.*
• *Emphasize description rather than interpretation.*
• *Practice empathy.*
• *Treat your interpretation as a working, open hypothesis.*

Our review of these points brought a vibrant "aha" from the participants.

Do you agree with this group's four rules (tools)? Before you answer consider the following fact: Each day we arrive at our employer's doorstep with our personal, invisible suitcase.

Let's pretend that this is your suitcase. You look inside and begin to marvel at what you discover. The items are all neatly folded and easily accessible. You invite us to look inside the suitcase with you. Here are our findings:

- On the bottom is a layer of homogenous language. You stand firm that English is the native language of these United States.

- Next you find cultural norms that span the spectrum from what is the meaning of the word "fair" to single-scope interpretations of non-verbal communication cues.

- Nestled on the right hand side of the next layer are our devout rules regarding work ethics.

- On the left hand side are Aunt Myra's wise old sayings. For example, "Hard work pays off in the long run." "Girls should be seen and not heard."

- Finally, the top layer is crowded with personal ethics, the rules that you impose on yourself. These rules are based upon the theories of ethical relativism. In other words, you firmly believe that what is considered to be ethical depends upon several variables; e.g., culture, tradition, background.

Now that we have had a look inside your invisible suitcase, please answer the previous question. Do you agree with the group's assessment? Caution: The four tools take an investment of time and a commitment to understanding.

> *"Leadership is an expression of a value set."*
> —*Nirenberg*

We live in an information and data-driven society. Data is easily available by depressing a few keystrokes anytime of the day or night. We seek trending data to assist with our business and career forecasts and decisions. I chuckle to myself as I figuratively travel back in time to my high school years. The high school counselor was the keeper of career data. It was shared with a student by appointment only. Imagine in your mind's eye:

> *It is a clear autumn afternoon. I sit across the desk from the counselor assigned to my group. She looks at me with a furrowed brow, with her glasses perched upon the tip of her nose. She smiles slightly as the words 'nurse, teacher, or secretary' are enunciated.*

I smile today because I am glad—no, I am ecstatically happy—that I did not listen to her.

Therefore, the following are workplace trending facts for consideration in our quest to understand diversity:

• As more women are added to the labor force, their share will approach that of men. In 2008, women will make up about 48 percent of the labor force and men 52 percent. In 1988, the respective shares were 45 and 55 percent." (Source: U.S. Department of Labor: Women's Share of Labor Force.)

• Employers will be unable to meet the flexibility requirements of many women. Women-owned businesses will become the career of choice for many women. Women-owned employer firms grew by 37 percent from 1997 to 2002, four times the growth rate of all employer firms.

• Emerging workplace trends as reported in a news release by ASTD (American Society of Training and Development) (1/15/04):

  - Technological advances are transforming the way we live and work

- Changing workforce characteristics and demographics means accommodating new attitudes, lifestyles, values, and motivations

- Increased globalization means more organizations are taking work off-site and off-shore

- Accelerated pace of change means organizations are becoming more flexible, networked, flat, diverse, and virtual

- Renewed focus on workplace ethics and trust calls into question the integrity of management and leadership

It is a fact that women, minorities, and immigrants are over 80 percent of the new entrants to the workforce (Leach, 1995). In addition, the people in positions of power within an organization, the dominant culture, may or may not be from the majority culture, the group with the largest numbers. Also, many people still believe that equal treatment equates to equality. In fact, equal treatment does not guarantee equality.

Today's business imperatives demand individual and organization paradigm shifts. A successful business lexicon includes the following terms: community, fully participative, consensus building, shared power, and collaboration. Therefore, each emerging professional must embrace the fact that each individual adds value by their unique contributions.

As a 'budding' professional woman, you may see leading an organization on your horizon. Realization of that dream requires the ability to communicate a clear vision of the future and inspire others to take action toward that vision. It requires facilitating change and taking advantage of opportunities to challenge old thinking, refocus individual and collective energies, and drive for results in new ways. It requires a mastery of diversity competencies.

R. Roosevelt Thomas, in his book *Building a House for Diversity*, (1999) defines core diversity skills as "the ability to recognize diversity mixtures, the ability to analyze the mixtures and related tensions, and the ability to select an appropriate response." The challenges facing you are many. For example:

- How will you bring people together to share their ideas, perspectives, and experiences?

- What is the impact of diversity mixtures on team dynamics?

- Do you understand what each of your key stakeholders are saying to you?

- Can you appropriately probe for information and clarity?

- Will you coach and initiate encouragement that meets the needs of each diverse receiver?

You are beginning to build a foundation for individual diversity accountability and responsibility. As you answer these questions, correlate the previous workplace trending facts to the intentions of your present and future workplace behaviors. Reminder: There is an impact of a leader's values, beliefs, and assumptions on all business decisions.

Career Success = Opportunity + Competency

Explore diversity as a professional competency!

We each view the world and the workplace through slightly different lenses; yet, there are some similarities. We are usually very comfortable acknowledging the similarities. Diversity tensions arise when there is no personal value acknowledgement of a different perspective. Your challenge is claiming (owning) responsibility for acquiring the knowledge and skills necessary to value different perspectives. This acquisition process begins with knowing yourself: your values and beliefs. Next steps include unlearning personal barrier perspectives—difficult to acknowledge and do.

Are you ready to become a champion for diversity? If your answer is, "I am not sure," consider the following messages of encouragement:

• Diversity is not a program. It is a mindset that triggers behaviors.

• Yes, "things" have changed in the last 25 years; however, the dynamics of diversity remain a critical business and personal success factor.

• The embracing of diversity clears the playing field for everyone to optimally utilize their skills for business and personal success.

• The embracing of the tenets of diversity creates an environment of inclusive excellence.

Joy Leach, author of *A Practical Guide for Working with Diversity* (AMACOM, 1995), states that there are emerging values for a diverse workplace. The old paradigm that includes hierarchy, exclusivity, and taking orders is on the way out. The new paradigm of community, inclusivity, and consensus are rebuilding the foundation of the workplace. We each must assess where we are on the understanding of diversity continuum.

"Cherish forever what makes you unique, 'cuz you're really a yawn if it goes!"
—*Bette Midler*

Resources

ASTD News Release. (1/15/04). *Emerging workplace trends signal changes for learning professionals.* Retrieved February 9, 2005.

Leach, J. (1995). *A practical guide to working with diversity.* New York: AMA COM, a division of American Management Association.

Nirenberg, John and Romine, Patrick. (2000). *The crafting of leadership: values, moral assumptions, and organizational change.* OD Practitioner, 32(2).

Thomas, R. R. (1999). *Building a house for diversity.* New York: AMACOM, American Management Association International.

ABOUT THE AUTHOR

KAREN DACE, PH.D.

A native of Chicago, Karen Dace attended the University of Illinois at Chicago where she received a Bachelor's degree in Liberal Arts and Master's degree in Communication. After working as a public relations account manager for three years in Chicago, she returned to college to pursue a doctorate in Communication Studies at the University of Iowa.

Karen Dace joined the faculty of the University of Utah in 1990 with a joint appointment in the Ethnic Studies Program and in the Department of Communication. She teaches and conducts research in intercultural communication, gender studies, conflict management, and group communication. During her tenure at the University of Utah, Professor Dace was named Director of the Ethnic Studies Program, an academic unit which houses and provides coursework in African American, American Indian, Asian Pacific American, and Chicana/o Studies. She has also served as Director of African American Studies.

In July 1999 Professor Dace was named the Associate Vice President for Diversity at the University of Utah. Her responsibilities include increasing the presence of women, people of color, persons with disabilities, and other under-represented groups on campus. In addition to coordinating celebration activities for Martin Luther King, Jr. and Women's Week, her office handles the annual Days of Remembrance which honors the more than six million Jews killed in the Holocaust. Both the Gender Studies and Ethnic Studies programs, as well as the American Indian Resource Center, American Indian Teacher Training Program, and the Center for Ethnic Student Affairs report to the Associate Vice President for Diversity.

In 2004, Dr. Dace launched The Dace Group, LLC, a diversity training and consulting group specializing in assisting corporations, schools, colleges and universities to explore ways to enhance their own diversity. She is a frequent keynote and guest speaker for agencies across the country.

Contact:
Karen L. Dace, President
The Dace Group
358 S. 700 East #B-219
Salt Lake City, Utah 84102
(801) 330-2414

TWENTY-ONE

FROM CHALLENGE TO OPPORTUNITY: MINORITY WOMEN IN THE WORKFORCE

By Dr. Karen Dace

Here is a challenge: write your life story. Here is an even greater challenge: write this story in a way that helps your readers understand the ways in which you experienced and enhanced diversity in the workplace. As someone preparing to or just entering the professional workforce, you may think your story too short to tell. You are correct. My challenge is that you think about what you would like your colleagues to remember about you when you retire. Specifically, how would you like them to describe your ability to work with individuals from diverse backgrounds, or from cultures not like your own? At the end of your career, what will you have accomplished to enhance your

own understanding of women from different races, ethnicities, economic and social classes, and religious backgrounds? Further, in what ways
will they say you improved the work environment for diversity?

I ask you to write your life story now because working effectively in
diverse environments requires some planning and thought. You cannot
expect to "fly by the seat of your pants" in the area of diversity if you
desire to be effective. If, at the end of your professional career, you want
your co-workers to say "she was an uncommon leader who made sure
that every voice was heard," or "she spoke up for me (or others) when no
one else would," or "she helped our company think about our differences
as a benefit and an opportunity rather than a problem," you will have to
make a conscious effort now to be that person.

Consider the remarks made at the end of your career should you not
opt to think creatively and proactively about diversity: "she was a great
boss except for people who were from a different background than
her own;" "you really couldn't count on her to take a stand around
multicultural issues;" "she avoided everyone who was not like her and
did her best to keep them silent."

All too often we think that the "burden" of educating the public
about multicultural issues should fall on the shoulders of those
traditionally viewed as diverse. Because of their religion, ethnicity, race,
or social standing, many women from diverse backgrounds have been
expected to help those from so-called mainstream backgrounds
understand them and their culture. Unfortunately, many women who
occupy the so-called mainstream often feel inadequate or believe they
have no responsibility at all to participate in creating understanding
between diverse cultures. Such situations and beliefs make understanding
and coalition building unlikely.

However, women from diverse backgrounds and those from what
has been traditionally identified as mainstream can and should work

together to create the dialogue and community that will benefit both groups and ultimately the workplace. As more women from every walk in life enter the work setting, more opportunities are created to learn about our differences and similarities. Further, there is tremendous evidence that different perspectives, growing out of our unique cultural backgrounds, contribute to improved problem-solving and decision-making. Many Fortune 500 companies understand this fact, especially as it relates to their bottom line—the better we understand diversity, the greater our profit. This is not to suggest that the only or most important benefit of understanding diverse cultures is financial. Rather, these benefits extend to expanding our understanding of those around us, creating feelings of appreciation and acceptance, and a welcoming office climate which can lead to greater job satisfaction and retention of employees.

What Would *You* Do?

To get you started on your journey to creating multicultural understanding in the workplace, here are some scenarios. Think about how you would respond, keeping in mind that your reaction will contribute to your life story.

Scenario I

> *You arrive early for a breakfast meeting and notice two people you have never met in the room. Before you can speak, your colleague and friend Mary Ann breezes in, nods in your direction, and heads toward the food. As she places fruit on her plate, she tells the woman standing near the beverage table "I'll have coffee, two sugars, and no cream." The woman, dressed in similar business casual attire, is a Latina. She very curtly explains, "While I work here, I am not a server, which is no doubt hard and honorable work. My name is Michele Flores and I work in Public Relations." Ms. Flores turns away abruptly, obviously*

upset. Over lunch, your friend complains "I don't know what the big deal was. It was an honest mistake. I don't know why she was so upset." How do you respond?

Scenario II

Your company pays for classes at a local college as long you can demonstrate the ways in which they will benefit you on the job. Which of the classes below would you be interested in taking? Which would you avoid? Why?

American History	American Indian Culture and Politics
Asian American Philosophy	Latino/Latina Political Movements
Mexican American History	African American Food and Music
Feminist Economics	The Lives and Philosophies of Martin Luther King and Malcolm X
Understanding Islam	The Politics of Judaism
Black Religion and Protest	Roots of American Culture
Jazz Traditions	Principles of Feminist Leadership
American Indian Religions	U.S. Popular Culture 1960-2000

Scenario III

You are in a planning meeting with your boss, a middle-aged, fair-minded man with whom you share the same race and social standing. The two of you are deciding whom in your division to invite to partici-pate in an exciting project that, if successful, would ensure the professional success of everyone involved. In fact, the national office of your company has promised that all who participate will be in line for a huge bonus and promotions into upper management. As your discussion draws to a close, you notice that everyone you plan to invite is also of the same race and social class as you and your boss. You also realize that there are several individuals in the division, representing different races and backgrounds, who would perform just as well as the individuals you have selected. Do you draw your boss's attention to this fact? Why? Why not? If you do decide to bring it up, what will you say to him?

Scenario IV

> *In the company cafeteria, you notice similar patterns of seating arrangements as you did in high school, and, to some extent, college. Most of the people are sitting in groups with others much like themselves. You notice that people of color are in one area, whites in another, and Muslims in yet another area. However, you have just concluded a very successful meeting with three other women. The four of you represent four different races and three religions. Your meeting was such a success that you decided to have a small celebration over lunch in the cafeteria. As you enter, pick up your trays and find a space at the end of one of the tables, you notice a strange quiet come over the room. All four of you are very aware of this silence and the fact that all eyes are on you. How do you feel? When you return to your office, what do you say to the co-worker who jokes, "Looks like you're starting your own little United Nations?" Will you eat with these women again?*

Some Food For Thought

Keep in mind, there are really no correct answers. In fact, there are very likely multiple appropriate responses for each scenario. Also, you will probably respond differently at different stages in your life and career. As your confidence builds, your responses may change. Hence, this section will not offer the answers as much as some issues to ponder as you contemplate these scenarios.

Scenario I – Clarification

Unfortunately, Latinos and other people of color, are often "mistaken" for "the help" in settings that are predominantly white. When this happens, it is problematic, disturbing, and annoying. Also, many people of color discuss their invisibility with co-workers when they are encountered both in the office and out. Women, regardless of their race, have experienced similar cases of "mistaken identity." For example, women in corporate settings complain about being expected to serve their male counterparts by running errands, getting coffee, and taking notes during meetings with men of equal status. Perhaps these common experiences may create space for discussion around this scenario.

Scenario II– Clarification

As a rule, any lecture, discussion, film, or class that sheds light on a culture with which you have little or no familiarity will benefit the company. This is especially true when those courses will help you understand your interactions with others or the reasons some people respond differently to the same issue. Further, because individuals viewed as "other" are often asked to explain their culture, it may be more thoughtful to take advantage of the wealth of information available through different outlets including documentaries, lectures, workshops and seminars. Such steps communicate genuine interest in different cultures. Finally, while courses focusing on food, festival and fun might be entertaining, unless your work requires dancing, singing, and eating different foods, classes focusing on music and food are probably unnecessary for corporate success.

Scenario III– Clarification

Again, the inclusion of individuals from different cultures brings perspectives that can only enhance discussion, interaction, and product. The promise of this project is too important—bonus and promotion— to risk including only those individuals with the same backgrounds and perspectives.

Scenario IV– Clarification

While initially uncomfortable, that feeling will pass. In fact, the four women in this scenario might use this as an opportunity to begin informal discussion groups to include diverse voices. The important question is not whether you would "eat with these women again." The important question is how will you feel about yourself if you avoid eating with women whose company you obviously enjoy?

Final Thoughts

Keep in mind that this is important and difficult work. The reason we choose to work on teams and have lunch with individuals much like ourselves is because of familiarity. There is a certain comfort in doing what we know and affiliating with people we can count on to share a common background. However, when we step out of our comfort zones and experience new ways of knowing and being, we not only learn new ideas, concepts, and perspectives, we learn more about ourselves. In work settings, this new information and understanding can lead to an improved office climate, more inclusive and creative decisions and products, and higher productivity.

In short, this work is not for the faint-of-heart. It takes courage to deal with an uncomfortable situation until it becomes more comfortable. It requires determination to question so-called office traditions in order to create a more inclusive work environment. Only thoughtful individuals can consider an unfair comment or situation and develop a way to approach the offender so that all parties come out as winners.

Now, unlike any time in our history, we have tremendous opportunities to bring greater understanding, appreciation, and acceptance of difference into our offices and communities. Perhaps you are the woman with that vision who can make it happen and write a life story that celebrates your contributions.

ABOUT THE AUTHOR

CAROL ANN RYSER, M.D.

Carol Ann Ryser, M.D. is a Board Certified Pediatrician (FAAP), Board Certified Clinical Analyst, member of: F.A.A.P., AMA, OHM (Orthomolecular Health Medicine), and The American Academy of Anti-Aging Medicine. The primary focus of Dr. Ryser's medical practice is on the prevention of illness and disease. As a physician, analyst, and practitioner of preventative medicine, Carol Ann Ryser has a broad background of experience, training, and knowledge to meet the demands of the 22nd century.

Dr. Ryser has published and presented a number of papers in her area of expertise, appearing in such publications as *The American Journal of Diseases of Children; Journal of Neurology, Neurosurgery and Psychology*; and *Pediatrics*. She has most recently published a chapter in the *Anti-Aging Medical Therapeutics Volume 5* entitled "Innovative Diagnosis and Treatment of Chronic Illness," *The Role of Growth Hormone Deficiency in Chronic Illness, Anti-Aging Medical News*, as well as several articles in alternative medical magazines.

Dr. Ryser has been a pioneer in the field of medicine since her graduation from KU Medical School in 1963. She was one of the first physicians to speak out against child abuse and helped change child abuse laws in the state of Kansas.

Dr. Ryser provides workshops, training seminars, and is a popular speaker throughout the United States. She speaks on medical issues concerning chronic illness; focusing on Lyme disease, Chronic Fatigue Syndrome, and Fibromyalgia, autoimmune diseases and preventative medicine, as well as self-esteem, psychotherapy, children, and child development. She serves as a Senior International Advisory Board member for The Professional Woman Network.

Contact:
Health Centers of America, KC, LLC
5308 E. 115th St., Kansas City, MO 64137-2731
(816) 763-9165
www.carolannrysermd.net
www.protrain.net

TWENTY-TWO

THE MIND–BODY CONNECTION

By Dr. Carol Ann Ryser

One of the great controversies of modern science is whether there exists a connection between the mind and the body. Scientists, physicians, biologist, chemists, physiologists, as well as the social scientific community—theologians, psychologists, and Eastern philosophical community—have long debated both sides of the paradox. However, based on current medical research, the new paradigm proposed by modern medical scientists, is a new term called "psychoneuro-immunology."

According to Candace B. Pert, Ph.D., in her book *Molecules and Emotion*, "Most psychologists treat the mind as disembodied, a phenomenon with little or no connection to the physical body. Conversely physicians treat the body with no regard to the mind or the emotions. But the body and mind are not separate, and we cannot treat one without the other. . . research has shown that the body can and must be healed through the mind and the mind can and must be healed through the body."

The concept of "psychoneuroimmunology," understanding the power of the mind and its effects on the function of the body, is a concept known by practitioners of faith, healers, psychology, and Eastern philosophy. The concepts of "mind over matter," "faith," "belief," and "willpower" have been accepted concepts for centuries by these groups. Most of the groups that espouse this concept have one anecdotal story after another to support their belief system.

A functional societal axiom is the belief that there must be a problem/illness before a plan is made to fix it. This has affected medicine in that until recently, modern medicine has not had a focus on "cause and effect" in relation to the mind and body. Because most of us operate or manage our lives by this type of crises management, modern medicine has been forced to re-think its position on how the mind influences the body and vice versa in order to solve many of the chronic illnesses we face in today's world.

It is important, not only in medicine, but in our everyday life, to learn to create a problem-solving philosophy that establishes a protocol of prevention. It is a known fact that our emotions/beliefs affect how we interpret scientific research and collect data, as well as how we stay healthy or become ill. It is also a known fact that we are affected by our lifestyle. One of the most important concepts we need to learn is to be aware of our own personal belief system that operates unconsciously and can influence our decision-making processes and ultimately, our well-being.

Now, modern medicine can also embrace this concept that the mind and body are intricately interwoven in their influence on each other. New research techniques and data can prove that there is a relationship between mind and body.

Many new models of addressing these issues have been created: hypnosis, cognitive therapy, acupuncture, electrical medicine, neurotherapy, cranial electrical stimulation, biomolecular medicine, psychotherapy, body therapies, energy medicine, homeopathy, orthomolecular and integrative medicine. These are all related to opening up the chemical and electrical systems of the body-mind functioning at the molecular level to recreate new options for health.

Understanding some of the basics of how our mind-body connection works will better enable a person to make personal changes. There are several theories of how we work. A creative researcher, Dr. Candice Pert, proved that there are molecules of emotion. She found a molecule on the surface of cells in the body and brain called the opiate receptor in 1972.

In regard to emotions, sleep deprivation, food deprivation, stress, trauma, infection, etc., can have a major effect on one's health and overall well-being. A good book to validate this is Norman Cousins' book, *Anatomy of an Illness.*

Paying attention to our emotions and expressing them in a therapeutic manner allows us to be integrated and whole. When our emotions are repressed we become blocked and ill.

A new look at molecules of emotions and how they affect who we are and what we are, is of utmost significance when looking at disease processes and aging.

The ultimate goal is to prevent aging diseases and degeneration such as cancer, immune system dysfunction, chronic infections, dementia, depression, early menopause, heart disease, diabetes, high blood pressure, osteoarthritis, osteoporosis, stroke, and morbid obesity by learning to attend to our health and body. Seventy to eighty percent of chronic illness is related to diet, lifestyle, poor nutrition, insomnia, depression, and emotional and physical stress.

The next consideration of how aging and chronic illness is related to the mind/body, is to understand three primary mechanisms of handling stress: cortisol, insulin, and neurotransmitters.

Cortisol

The first mechanism of managing stress to consider is **cortisol**. Cortisol is an active steroid hormone secreted in the greatest quantity by the adrenals and is the most potent of the naturally occurring glucocorticoids in humans. One of the benefits of cortisol is that it is an antiflammatory. It is one of the major stress-regulating hormones of the body. If it malfunctions, it can be a death hormone.

Function of cortisol:

- Maintains blood pressure from being too low. Low blood pressure causes hypoxia (low oxygen) occurring in the brain, heart, pancreas, other organs.

- Maintains water balance.

- Stores glycogen, a hormone that regulates sugar in the liver and maintains blood sugar, thus preventing hypoglycemia (low blood sugar).

- Mobilizes energy for the brain by maintaining adequate sugar levels. If low blood sugar occurs, then the body:
  1. Breaks down protein (it is converted to sugar to save the brain).
  2. Blocks uptake of sugar to muscles by shifting glucose to the brain and pancreas.
  3. Breaks down fats to glycerol and fatty acids, which can be converted to sugar.
  4. Protects fat in the brain from being used as fuel, mobilizes peripheral proteins, and fats for energy. The brain is ninety percent cholesterol and fatty acids.

- Helps fight inflammation by fighting off viruses, bacteria, foreign proteins, i.e. reduces inflammation response.

- Responds to acute stress: increases blood pressure, activates energy, keeps body warm, and feeds the brain with sugar

Causes of Low Cortisol:

• Addison's disease – autoimmune destruction of adrenal gland

• Secondary adrenal insufficiency – related to pituitary and ACTH hormone

• Congenital adrenal hypoplasia - (glands not formed)

• Surgical removal

• Adrenal gland destruction caused by lymphoma, infections, hemorrhages

• Trauma

• Drugs (antifungal Ketoconazole)

• Chronic infections: viral, bacterial, fungal, spirochete

• Hypercoagulation state – excessive clotting decreases oxygen to the body

• Anti-seizure medication: Dilantin, Phenobarbital

• Rifampin – anti-tuberculosis drug

Causes of High Cortisol:

• Benign tumor
• Cancer
• Congenital Hyperplasia
• Glucocorticoid steroids - Prednisone
• Chronic stress
• Chronic infection with clotting disorder
• Prescription drugs

Cortisol is necessary for survival. High ongoing cortisol is considered the destructive death hormone. Low cortisol causes extreme fatigue and inability to respond to stress. A person's lifestyle affects the level of cortisol.

1) Nutritional deficiency and restriction of calories creates a deficiency that causes thyroid hypo-function.

2) Exposure to chemicals damages the body's balance. An example is that alcohol and drugs block the liver from the breaking down glucose into sugar for the brain. Also cortisol breaks down proteins and fats to make sugar to be used when under stress, but can damage cells.

3) Physiologic stress and excess exercise cause oxidative, physiological stress that damages cells and causes cell death.

4) Hormonal stress. Hormone deficiency is essential for balanced body function.

5) Emotional stress can create an imbalanced life style that prevents one from taking care of a healthy lifestyle such as adequate sleep, exercise, good nutrition, supportive relationships, and creative work.

Initially, excessive chronic stress and infection can cause an increase in cortisol. Later however, it can cause depletion of cortisol. Under excessive stress, cortisol is secreted from the adrenal gland and is required to manage the following situations:

• Depression: mental concern, worrying about finances, relationships, upcoming surgery, etc.

• Hypomania: doing too many things or not setting limits

• Exposure to cold

• Chronic infection

• Chronic pain and tension

• Over-functioning with loss of sleep, rest, good nutrition, relaxation,

• Exposure to physical and emotional threats

• Trauma: physical injury, severe burns, surgery, inflammation

• Significant losses: divorce, death of a loved one, financial losses, etc.

Insulin

The second mechanism to manage stress is **insulin**. Insulin is another hormone that reacts to our body's environment. It is produced by the pancreas and is one of the most sensitive organs to hypoxia (lack of oxygen). Chronic low insulin is just as harmful as chronic high insulin.

Your survival depends on your ability not to waste away or become obese. Eating a balanced meal of protein, good fats, vegetables, real carbohydrates (fruits and vegetables) protects you. Do not skip meals. This creates a stress reaction. Do not eat high carbohydrates or low-fat diet. Low insulin causes your body to use up your protein, fats, and causes you to waste away.

High adrenalin and high insulin cause the same deficiency state as that of low insulin. This is the stress reaction that causes deficient metabolism and leads to disease. The causes of low insulin levels are low-calorie diet, excessive high proteins, excessive carbohydrates, starvation, excessive dieting and anoxia.

These can lead to disease states: fatigue, thyroid disease, susceptibility to infections, hypoglycemia, diabetes, and depression. The body has a mechanism for handling the damage of too much sugar. Excess sugar is converted to two types of fat: cholesterol and triglycerides. A lack of exercise also contributes to this conversion. Refined sugar is actually more damaging to the body than high fats. Thus eat whole grains, legumes, starchy vegetables, and fruit, along with good monosaturated fats and protein.

Insulin and a balanced diet help the body get enough sugar to the cells and the brain, for functioning. Excessive sugar damages brain cells. One can see the importance of the mind-body connection being controlled by our diet. The body requires energy to function. Brain cells, red blood cells, special cells in your kidneys can only use sugar.

Other cells can use sugar and fat (ketone). After 72 hours of low sugar, the body switches to ketones that can be destructive to your body functions. Many medical tests are designed to evaluate abnormal sugar metabolism, levels of cholesterol, hormones, sugar and insulin function. When an imbalance occurs, destructive processes begin in our body that lead to brain, hormone, energy, and circulation dysfunction.

Insulin sensitivity is normal and aids the following activities:
• Sugar is taken up by the liver for conversion to energy.
• Excessive sugar is converted to high triglycerides and cholesterol.
• Excessive cholesterol and triglycerides are taken in by the body's cells and stored.
• Sugar must go into the cells to drive the energy function of cells.

When sugar is used in cells, insulin levels returns to normal. The process starts over when you eat. Insulin fluctuation is not usually felt unless excessive carbohydrates are eaten. Signs of excessive fluctuation of insulin are:

• Clammy skin	• Heart palpitations	• Light-headedness
• Fatigue	• Sugar cravings	• Foggy thinking
• Panic attacks	• Sleeping after eating	• Insomnia
• Irritability	• Loose bowel movement	

The ultimate malfunction comes from years of excessive carbohydrates. The cells become filled with fat, and the insulin no longer works to get sugar to the cells and your body is on the way to becoming insulin resistant. Symptoms of insulin resistance are:

• Acne	• Infections
• Ankle swelling	• Irregular menses

- Alternating constipation and digestion
- Decrease memory/concentration
- Depression
- Fatigue
- High blood pressure
- Elevated triglycerides
- Irritability
- Burning feet
- Water retention
- Weight gain
- Foggy brain

Years of abnormal dietary habits and inactivity create insulin resistance. Syndrome X, or insulin resistance, is manifested by elevated insulin, obesity, and hypertension, and elevated triglycerides. Elevation of triglycerides also occurs with smoking, stress, birth control pills, and alcohol.

Medical conditions that occur with high insulin, in addition to Syndrome X, are:

- Elevated lipid profile: high triglycerides, low HDL (good cholesterol), elevated LDL (bad cholesterol)
- Hypertension
- Type II diabetes
- Coronary atherosclerosis
- Cerebral atherosclerosis
- Cancers, especially of breast, prostate, colon
- Stein-Leventhal Syndrome, infertility, anovulatary menstrual cycle, no periods, abdominal fat, acne/facial hair

Cholesterol (the most abundant steroid in animal tissue) serves several important functions in the body:

- Forms insulation around nerves so they can fire
- Maintains healthy immune cells
- Aids the integrity of cell membranes

- Keeps cell membranes flexible and permeable
- Aids brain function
- Makes body hormones: estrogen, progesterone, testosterone, and steroids

Neurotransmitters

The third mechanism to manage stress is **neurotransmitters.** An important link in our disease versus health is the availability of brain biochemicals, called neurotransmitters. Our busy lifestyle burns or uses up all neurotransmitters. This deficient state can be induced by all the stresses that are influenced by hormones, the endocrine system, diet, emotional stress, environment toxins, alcohol, cigarettes, some drugs, chronic infection, insomnia, clotting or circulation problems, and the list goes on.

One such neurotransmitter is serotonin. When serotonin is low, feelings of unhappiness and anxiety occur as well as lack of calmness (anxiety). Intermittent low serotonin may produce body aches and pains, cravings for sugar, alcohol, cigarettes, caffeine and recreational drugs, fatigue, intestinal bloating/indigestion, irritability, insomnia, depressed mood and poor memory/concentration. Disorders of serotonin deficiency are as follows:

• Chronic fatigue syndrome	• Fibromyalgia	• Obesity
• Migraine headaches	• Depression	• Sleep disorder
• Seasonal affective disorder	• Premenstrual syndrome	

We attempt to solve these problems by developing addictive behaviors. A vicious cycle occurs when diets contain excessive sugar or inadequate calories, and artificial sweetener (Aspartame-Nutrasweet blocks the enzyme that makes serotonin); diets that cause vitamin D-deficiency or lack of sunshine; diets that encourage poor intake of good fats and proteins; diets that cause low estradiol, unhealthy adrenals, and thyroid.

Serotonin comes from an essential amino acid called tryptophan. Tryptophan is found in peanuts, cottage cheese, almonds, oatmeal, soy food, tuna, and turkey. The biochemical pathways that use tryptophan require insulin, thyroid, calcium, magnesium, essential fatty acids, vitamin C, B vitamins, and hormones. Serotonin becomes melatonin at night or in dark environments. Melatonin is an anti-aging hormone that helps with sleep. Ways to regenerate serotonin are to eat a balanced diet (avoid excess carbohydrates), get adequate light, have relaxation time, meditation, play, laughter, reading, massage, get adequate sleep, exercise (not over-exercise), and deal with excessive anger (this also depletes serotonin).

Hormone replacement therapy helps conserve serotonin. Long-term birth control usage blocks estradiol function and creates a major serotonin deficiency syndrome.

Ways to balance your mind body function are related to the interplay of many factors. Adrenaline (or epinephrine) is a catecholamine that is the chief neurohormone of the adrenal medulla, and is secreted by neurons. It is one of the most important factors that responds to stress, thereby affecting the mind-body balance.

In summary, the following are examples of what happens when each of these three mechanisms for managing stress are out of control, thereby leading to medical and emotional problems.

Ways that cortisol is triggered:

• Low carbohydrate intake, starvation

• Missing meals

• Dieting

- Chronic stress
- Lack of sleep
- Alcohol
- Cigarettes
- Excessive exercise
- Use of glucosteroids
- Emotional stress
- Chronic inflammation
- Clotting, lack of oxygen
- Chronic infection
- Loss of sex hormones
- Loss of human growth hormone, DHEA, thyroid
- Physical trauma, surgery, accidents

Ways that insulin is triggered:
- Excessive carbohydrates
- Unbalanced meals
- Inflammation
- Clotting problem/circulation

Ways that excessive adrenaline is triggered:
- Skipping meals or excessive carbohydrates
- Dieting
- Low-carbohydrate diet
- Excessive protein intake
- Excessive refined sugar ("white stuff")

• Stimulants-caffeine, cigarettes

• Birth control pills

• Menopause (low estradiol)

• Synthetic provera and premarin

• Excessive DHEA and testosterone

In conclusion, when you are ready to change your life stresses, it is important to make a decision to take charge of the process. There are several things you can do to help yourself with decision making. First, it is critical to educate yourself. The more information you have about yourself, especially your beliefs about how the world works, about your health, and your relationships, the more options you have about what decisions to make. Second, seek professional help. When you believe you are out of options or "stuck" in your decision making, a professional can help you change and reach your potential. Third, learn to confront yourself with new options, change your way of thinking and your belief system that is holding you back. You may also want to seek medical advice and evaluate your stress hormones and biochemical balance.

You can change. It is never too late and you can never run out of options to change your thoughts, feelings, behaviors and belief system. Your physical health, your emotional health, and your spiritual health are all related to making the right decisions *right now*. Ask yourself this question, "Where will I live if my body is destroyed?"

There are some anti-aging secrets that will help your mind work better, help your body to slow down the aging process, and enhance prevention of disease and illness. Those secrets are as follows:

• Following a balanced nutrition plan.

• Taking the correct and most bio-available supplements.

- Finding an exercise program that you will follow.

- Getting adequate sleep.

- Maintaining hormone balance. Consider seeing a physician who can help when your system is out of balance. Find a physician who will help with natural hormone replacement when needed.

- Creating and maintaining healthy relationships that are supportive to you and supportive of your changing.

- Drinking adequate water (dehydration causes and exacerbates illness).

- Eliminating toxins from your body and stop taking alcohol, drugs, cigarettes, etc.

- Giving yourself permission to be healthy and creative.

- Treating infections and circulatory disorders.

Planning to stay healthy, youthful, and slowing down the aging process longer than you have ever imagined can go a long way to improve your quality of life. It is important to have extended longevity as a personal goal, as well to support longevity in medical science and society in general. The goal is not only to live longer but to live a vigorous life in full possession of your faculties, powers, financial security, and personal freedom.

What meaning will we give to our lives? What adjustments in our commitments, priorities, and ambitions will we have to make? How will our marriage, children, friendships, and professional relationships evolve? What energy and resources will we access to make a change in our mental, physical and spiritual health? That is the purpose of this chapter, to help you think about these questions and create healthy options for your life.

And as the question was asked before: "Where will you live if your body is destroyed?" The choice is yours.

Resources

Eat Right for Your Type, by Peter D. Adamo

Whole-Brain Thinking, by Priscillia Donova and Jacquelyn Wonder

Nutrients to Age Without Senility, by Abraham Hoffer, M.D. and Morton Walker, D.P.M.

Ortho-Molecular Nutrition, by Abraham Hoffer, M.D. and Morton Walker, D.P.M.

Nutrition and The Mind, by Gary Null, Ph.D.

Antiaging Secrets for Maximum Lifespan, by Ronald M. Katz, M.D.

How to Do Something About the Way You Feel, by David L. Messenger, M.D., and John C. Sauter

"OrthoMolecular, The Right Knowledge of the Right Nutrients", *Science ,* by Linus Pauling, 1968

Molecules of Emotion, by Candace R. Pert

Solved: The Riddle of Illness, by James F. Schele and Stephen E. Tanger, M.D.

The Schwarzbein Principal II, by Diana Schwarzbein, M.D.

Ten Weeks to a Younger You, by Ronald M. Klatz, M.D.

Biochemical Individuality, by Roger William, M.D.

ABOUT THE AUTHOR

DINA FINTA

Ms. Finta is CEO and owner of Momentum, a Louisiana-based business skills and technology company providing comprehensive training and consulting for business. Former COO of The Bierman Group, she is nationally recognized for her work in developing courseware and instruction tools in the areas of sales management, human resource management, technology upgrades, ethics, and marketing. She is a leading member of United Training and the Professional Woman Network International Advisory Board. She is a highly sought-after presenter in Customer Service, Leadership, Time Management, Communication Skills, Selling Skills, Team Building, Executive Coaching, and Personal Development training to widely disparate audiences.

Dina's workshops are tailored specifically to the goals and objectives of organizations of all sizes. Among her recent clients are: ChevronTexaco, Department of Revenue, United States Navy, Appro Systems, and Louisiana Division of Administration. Ms. Finta is a member of the National Speakers Association, makes conference appearances and delivers energetic keynote addresses. Ms. Finta has received numerous local, regional and national awards, and serves on a number of prestigious boards and organizations.

Contact:
Momentum
P.O. Box 87002
Baton Rouge, LA 70879
(225) 295-4150
dfinta@teammomentum.com
www.teammomentum.com
www.protrain.net

TWENTY-THREE

THE POWER OF YOU: MAKING A POSITIVE IMPACT

By Dina Finta

You're on the road now, and it's time to begin a new chapter of your life in the business world. The direction your life takes now is completely up to you—personally and professionally. You have the power to make a positive impact!

First, I commend you on your success so far. I hope in these few pages I can give you some guidance, a cheat sheet that I never had, to help you make a positive impact in the professional world. I have spent almost twenty years in the business world learning, making mistakes, taking risks, and experiencing both setbacks and victories. My goal is to help you avoid some of the mistakes I made and give you an inside track to success. The five impact points following detail the concepts I think are most important to a new business person. The trick for you will be applying these impact points to your situation; they may sound like common sense, but my experience is that the business people whom I admire most and are most successful are also the ones who most clearly, to me, demonstrate these principles.

The Five Impact Points (FIP)

1. You always have a choice.
2. Take control of your professional and personal development.
3. Understand the big picture and keep sight of your own goals.
4. Approach each day with a fresh outlook.
5. Look outside yourself.

Sounds simple right? We'll see!

You always have a choice.

Now more than ever before, you are responsible for the choices in your life. Before now you were probably dependent on the direction of others such as parents and then your teachers or college professors. But now it's all you. If you are already in a professional job, then you have made a choice. This is the real deal. Someone has chosen to hire you as part of their company. This may be a larger concept than you realize! Every time a hiring decision is made, it impacts not only your personal life but the entire company. The best thing I can do in my own business is to hire people who can bring different strengths to the company. You were hired because you can potentially do that in your new role. When a job offer is made, points such as salary and benefits are discussed with you upfront. These things are not surprises. If you don't feel like this is a good move or a good fit for you, then don't take the position—it is your choice.

If you decide to take a job, seize it and bring your best to it every day. By the way, I hope you've chosen a job that you find interesting and potentially fulfilling. You will be more motivated and successful if you enjoy what you are doing. I majored in Fashion Merchandising at Louisiana State University. I accepted my first job at a privately owned specialty department store based in Birmingham, Alabama. I was offered a job in their Management Training Program and quickly discovered that I had a lot to learn. I learned especially that one's choice of a job is only the first choice. The decision to carry on every day, to give your best work every day, to work toward your goals every day, those are choices you make daily. Right or wrong, you make them daily.

Take control of your personal and professional development.

Ever listen to guys in a gym? They have a thing they like to yell on heavy lifts: "All you! All you!" In business it really is "all you." I look back at some of my earlier jobs and know I could have performed better. I didn't always take the initiative and the responsibility (or have the knowledge!) to develop myself. In my first job at Parisian Inc., I was fortunate to work for a wonderfully successful woman. Linda Green was my first role model in the business world. She instilled in me the passion to reach new heights in my professional life, but as importantly, she made it all up to me. I needed to live the role I wanted to achieve. In my case, because I wanted to be like Linda, I began to act like her from a professional standpoint. I observed, learned and eventually modeled my management style after her. She expected high performance from her team and effectively motivated us by being a leader we wanted to follow.

In our lives we all look to successful people for guidance. I share a passion for continuous learning. Ever read Jack Welch or Oprah Winfrey? You should. By any measure they are at the top of their field, and constantly site the importance of owning your own growth. I have a kind of wacky method for my own personal and professional development. I choose three books every time I go to the library: a business book, a fiction book, and an autobiography. People like Catherine Wright (sister to the famous Wright brothers), Mary Shelley (the author of *Frankenstein*) and Abraham Lincoln have amazing relevance to modern business, if you're in the right frame of mind. Many spectacularly successful business people have written books or at least have had biographies written about them; Warren Buffett, Bill Gates, Oprah Winfrey—all amazing people. I really cannot overemphasize the importance of general professional reading. Force yourself to branch out into uncommon territory. Stretch yourself professionally, seek risk and uncomfortable situations. If you're comfortable in your job, you're not growing. Professionally, look for ways to increase your knowledge at work. Find people who hold positions you would like to have someday. Ask them for guidance. Take them to lunch and ask them for advice on how to follow that career path. Find mentors outside your own company as well. Some of my current professional mentors have a variety of backgrounds and experiences. Jim, my husband, who is a military officer, has helped me consider things from the viewpoint of a large, very structured organization. Tom Finta, my father-in-law, is a retired Navy captain and is now the CEO of a small company. The breadth of his background helps me every time I talk with him. Todd Shelton is a small company entrepreneur and CEO in my same industry. Todd can relate to my challenges, has sometimes made the mistakes before I have, and always offers me a fresh outlook. My parents laid the groundwork for my core values of ethics, honesty, and integrity.

Who are your mentors now? Who are you emulating? You may also choose to pattern yourself after other business people that you don't know.

Networking is another of your critical professional development tools. Volunteer to attend after-hours business mixers through organizations like your local Chamber of Commerce. Find special interest groups in your particular field. Networking events can be uncomfortable (discomfort means you're growing!) but are great places to meet your colleagues and enhance both your professional acumen and your contact list. You have nothing to lose and a lot to gain. Savern Varnado, a close colleague of mine and a great personal friend, likens the situation to the sports world. One of his favorite sayings is "Take the shot!" If you don't step out and put yourself in uncomfortable situations then you are stifling your growth. No one is going to drag you out to business events, no one is going to put books in your hand or take any more interest in your career than you do. Take control!

Understand the big picture.

So many times we focus on achieving a small specific goal but have no idea how this task affects the bigger picture. What is the big picture for your company, for your family, and for yourself? If you understand the goals and expectations of your employer and understand how you can impact his/her achievement of these goals, then of course you are able do better work. I firmly believe that the single greatest factor in uninspired performance is a fundamental misunderstanding of how a task or job fits the bigger job. Some business books call it "following the company blueprint." As a new retail manager, I always thought about my immediate area of responsibility—in my case, the Children's Division. I had very little knowledge of the operation of the company in general, or of how my little section affected that operation. Looking back now, I can see a myriad of opportunities that my understanding might have opened up. That is why in my consulting business today, my first task is understanding the overall company I'm working with, and specifically how the service I offer can help that company or department, or even the individual, work toward that goal. That is your task. Research the background of the company you work for and figure out what the big picture is. Where do they want to be in one year, or in five years? Ask your supervisor what her goals are in one year, five years or beyond. How does the task you do every day help her achieve this goal? This is how you can personally impact the big picture. The most valuable members of my team ask these questions and understand exactly what my vision is for the company. They help me work toward my vision every day and are the team members I can't do without. This is the place you want to be.

Goals, goals, goals! Do you make a New Year's resolution? Do you keep it? As a kid, my whole family would privately write down our resolutions each year and put them in a jar. The following year, we would pull the jar out and see if we kept it. Well, as you probably guessed, most years we didn't keep the resolution and some years we couldn't even find the jar. Not how I recommend goal tracking! The first step is determining and writing down your goals but the second part of the task is to keep them in front of you! At the end of this chapter, take a few minutes and write down two personal and two professional goals. Keep the personal goals at home on your mirror, in your car, or on your refrigerator. I even encourage my 13-year-old son, Cale, to update his own personal goals at the beginning of each school year. If he doesn't understand what those goals are, he won't reach them. Your professional objectives should also be in a visible location. I always have my sales team keep their goals or their focus clients posted on their bulletin boards so they see them many times throughout the day and are more likely to put efforts toward them. Make sure your goals are concise, measurable and achievable (but aggressive)!

Approach each day with a fresh outlook.

Hard times are growth times. Let's be honest! Work can become monotonous as time passes. It's easy to put in your time and go home and enjoy a moderate amount of success. The fact that you're reading a book about developing yourself professionally tells me that you're not satisfied with that. OK, now keep that dissatisfaction up for your entire career, and I guarantee you that you will outperform most of your colleagues. You can still do the same things you are doing today again tomorrow and approach them with a fresh outlook. I constantly ask my team, especially those who have been with me for more than two years, to act like today is their first day on the job. The difference is that they now know the company and their job really well and their competence levels are probably much higher than they were when they started. So with this knowledge, go into work with a fresh outlook. Some business books estimate that it only takes six months to become so much a part of a system that you cannot see it as a whole. Fight that! In my company, we have all-hands meetings twice a week–we call these "fishbowl" meetings. The team meets in one central spot and we discuss the day's focus, and how we can make the client experience better today than ever before. It doesn't cost money—it's an attitude and it makes all the difference in the world. So make the commitment today to approach tomorrow like a brand-new, but highly informed employee.

Surround yourself with positive people. Think about the most negative person you know...now think about the most positive. Now (more frightening) if your colleagues were asked to do the same, would any think of you? You have the opportunity to choose your friends; you probably don't have the ability to pick your co-workers. But, you can choose whom to emulate and associate with at work; they should be people who make you feel positive about your job and yourself. Find a role model at work and choose to spend your time with him or her.

One of the most positive people I know is my 13-year-old sister-in-law Katya. She is a (very good) gymnast who's had some (VERY) bad luck in her career: a broken neck and a broken collar bone in one year alone. Yet even in the midst of her pain and discomfort, she always had a positive outlook. She appreciated that she wasn't more severely injured, and that's not easy to focus on, especially at her age. Even though her gymnastics career could have been over, there were still so many other positive things that held her focus. She is always a pleasure to be with, and her attitude gives her charisma. I am sure that she will have a successful career in whatever she chooses.

Look outside yourself.

I feel passionately about this. You have the power to make a positive impact in somebody else's life. You don't have to give money—in fact, in many cases, your commitment of time can make an even bigger impact. My favorite quote is by Gandhi: "You must be the change you wish to see in the world." Even the smallest outreach effort can make a difference in the lives of others. As a business person, you will benefit by staying in contact with your community. As a person, you will benefit from looking outside yourself and your worklife stresses and concerns. My company volunteers time and money to the local battered women's shelter. I even allow my team to use up to 40 hours a year of work time to do volunteer work. This time is paid because I really believe as a small business owner that I have the obligation to give back to the community. If we all made a small commitment, what a difference we could make!

This is all up to you now. Good luck! Give it your best! Use the worksheet on the next page to help you clarify your goals!

Describe your personal "big picture" goals.

Think about what goals you can reach in the next six months, in the next month, today. To reach your goals, they must first be clearly identified. Set the goal, then list three things you can do today to work toward that goal.

Goal:_____

1._____

2._____

3._____

Now, describe the "big picture" goals of your company and then of your supervisor. If you are having trouble, ask for clarification.

_____

_____

_____

3. List three things you can do today to shape your efforts to meet these larger goals. Small planned actions will help you accomplish these goals more effectively.

1._____

2._____

3._____

Name the most negative person you know:_____

Name the most positive person you know:_____

Think about the traits of the people listed above. What traits would others list when describing your attitude? List three actions you can take to help you take a positive approach personally.

1._____

2._____

3._____

List three actions you can take to help you take a positive approach professionally. Work these actions into your day tomorrow, then think of three more to do next week. Continue to plan these actions to ensure your continuous development.

1._____

2._____

3._____

To enhance your professional development, research and list two professional organizations in which you can get involved. Make immediate plans to attend their next function. This will be a great way to meet new business people and possibly another mentor.

1._____

2._____

If you already have mentors, list them below. If not, think of two people who would fit this role for you on a personal level.

1._____

2._____

List two people who would fit this role professionally.

1._____

2._____

Start to spend more planned time with the mentors you have listed above. Ask them for advice; ask them what they do for professional development.

Notes:

ABOUT THE AUTHOR

HAZEL BLAKE PARKER

Hazel Blake Parker is Chief Executive Officer of The Parker Institute for Excellence, LLP, and Director of Staff Development and Training for the South Carolina Department of Social Services (DSS). She has gained extensive knowledge and experience in management, training, and family life issues through these positions. She has developed, coordinated, facilitated, and evaluated training sessions for groups that have included all levels of staff from administrative assistants to executive staff.

Ms. Parker established The Parker Institute for Excellence, LLP in 2001 to provide personal and professional development training seminars to all types of organizations. Topics include Conflict, Time and Stress Management, Parenting, Effective Supervision, Leadership, Enhancing Family Strengths, and Self-Esteem. She also conducts grant writing workshops, writes and reviews proposals for nonprofit organizations, and assists organizations in obtaining nonprofit status. She has been a Certified Grant Writer since 1998.

As Training Director, Ms. Parker develops and monitors over $6 million in training contracts and manages over 20 staff responsible for training about 4,000 DSS employees statewide. Ms. Parker has worked for the agency for over 21 years in various capacities, from frontline caseworker to manager. She is also involved in many organizations and a member of the International Board of Advisors for the Professional Woman Network. She resides in Orangeburg, South Carolina with her husband, Terry and son, Taurean.

Hazel Blake Parker

Contact:
The Parker Institute for Excellence, LLP
P.O. Box 2438
Orangeburg, SC 29116
(803) 347-5627
parkerinstitute@oburg.net
www.parkerinstitute.com
www.protrain.net

TWENTY-FOUR

LIFE ORGANIZATION & PRIORITIZING

By Hazel Blake Parker

Women. The thread of life. They hold together every major institution known to man—families, friendships, and workplaces. They have planned meals, birthday parties, and weddings for family and friends while conducting office meetings, compiling reports, and troubleshooting problems at work. Managing multiple roles has become a way of life for the average woman, especially now that almost two-thirds of adult women participate in the labor force. Balancing work, family, and social activities effectively and efficiently can be quite a feat. As women, we tend to want the best for our family and friends, while neglecting our own needs and desires. We must learn to organize and prioritize our life tasks if we are to overcome this tendency to constantly give and do for others.

The goal of this chapter is to help you prioritize and organize your life's tasks so that you gain control of your time and live life with more balance and satisfaction. We will examine how you prioritize five basic

289

life categories—work, family, friends, health, and spirit—and provide practical tips and techniques to help you prioritize and get organized, both at home and at work. Throughout the chapter you'll be given many opportuities to reflect upon many aspects of your life and at the end, you'll be asked to develop an action plan for organizing and prioritizing your life.

Let's begin by looking at your priorities. Reflect upon your life currently and rank the following categories in priority order from 1 to 5, with 1 being the top priority.

> ### Categories of Life Activities
> _____ Work
> _____ Family
> _____ Friends
> _____ Spirituality
> _____ Health

While there is no "correct" order, by the end of the chapter you'll see that some are indeed more important than others. We will revisit this list again before you develop your action plan.

When well-managed, multiple life roles can be complimentary and lead to a fulfilling life. However, when roles get out of balance, stress levels rise and health problems may result, causing detrimental effects at work and at home. In order to lead a more balanced life, you must plan, prioritize, and organize. Let's begin by taking a look at how you spend your time. List the ten tasks that consume most of your time on a weekly basis. If making this list proves difficult, consider keeping a journal to capture such information.

10 Most Time-Consuming Tasks

1._____

2._____

3._____

4._____

5._____

6._____

7._____

8._____

9._____

10._____

• How many were work-related? _____

• How many pertained to family issues? _____

• How many were socially oriented? _____

• How many related to your top-ranked life category?_____

• Which tasks on your list would you like to spend the most time on?

    • _____

    • _____

    • _____

• What tasks are not listed that you would like to be on the list?

    • _____

    • _____

    • _____

Now, review your list and the answers to the above questions.

• Why aren't you spending more time on those things that you prefer to do? _____
_____

• What is keeping you from doing the tasks that did not make your list?

_____

_____

_____

The Road to an Organized Life

Personal Priorities

The first and most important thing you can do to organize your life is to determine your personal priorities. Once you've done this, then everything else can be put into perspective. Without knowing what your priorities are, you'll continue to let trivial matters and other people take control of your time. The following will help you begin this process:

What people/relationships do you value most?

_____

_____

_____

What are your personal goals? (List your top three.)

_____

_____

_____

What is getting in the way of you reaching these goals?

_____

_____

_____

The answers to these questions will also help you clarify your values so that you can weigh the worth of activities in which you participate. *Efficient* use of time doesn't necessarily mean *effective* use of time. If you have filled up your schedule and squeezed in all of the things you think you need to do, but haven't done anything that you wanted to do, then you have efficiently, but ineffectively, planned your time. Plan your time with intention so that you can take your values into account. Schedule those things that mean the most to you first and then schedule other activities only if you have sufficient time and the desire to do them. Recognize that we all have to be flexible. There will be times when situations arise that require our immediate attention. Don't let them entirely derail your plans. Simply look at the other activities you have planned and re-prioritize them according to your needs.

Getting to 'No'

Another very important aspect of life organization and prioritizing, especially for women, is the inability to say "no." We often overextend ourselves by volunteering for too many church, school, or social committees —all the while working full-time and maintaining a household. When asked to participate in an activity, remember your personal priorities and evaluate the request. If it does not qualify as a priority for you, just say no. The problem with saying no is the guilty feelings often associated with it. We feel as if we have to justify our no to alleviate the guilt. Instead of feeling guilty, take pride in the fact that you're taking control. It does, however, take getting used to. The more you say no, the easier it will become. What is it costing us *not* to say no?

• Lack of control over our time

• Loss of self-esteem

• Health problems, stress, etc.

• Missed deadlines

Over time and in extreme situations, conceding to others' desires can even lead to abuse. You can get so wrapped up pleasing others that you are soon being totally controlled by someone else. Remember, the choice is yours. Saying no to others is saying yes to yourself.

Get Control of Your Time

Take ownership of your time. Don't allow others to set your schedule or plan your life. Always reflect upon your list of priorities and values before embarking upon any mission that is not yours. While we can't shut everybody and all outside activities out of our lives, we can limit the amount of time we spend on them. If you think about an average day, you may find that precious little time was spent on leisure activities or self-care. We simply fill up our days with tasks that benefit everybody but us. Make some "me" time every day, even if it's only 15 or 30 minutes. Here are a few tips on how you can find that all-important "me" time:

• **Get up 15 to 30 minutes earlier.** Take this time to meditate, read, write in your journal, listen to music, or just sit and relax. This will help you get your day off to a positive start and put you in a more relaxed frame of mind.

• **Enjoy a hobby.** Engaging in activities such as reading, crossword puzzles, crafts, etc., can help you tune out the world temporarily and focus on that one thing. If you enjoy the outdoors, take up hiking or gardening. A hobby clears the mind of the work–life clutter that seems to clog our heads, thus reducing our stress levels and improving our overall attitude. Be sure that your hobby fits your personality, abilities ,and budget.

• **Make a personal care appointment.** Get your hair done, a manicure, pedicure, massage, etc. The time and monetary commitment involved increases the likelihood that you'll follow through with it. Relax and enjoy the pampering. This, too, is a stress reliever as you receive individual attention without having to do anything in return.

• **Take a class.** Enroll in a community interest course, such as cake decorating, yoga, self-improvement, or any topic of interest offered in your community. These classes usually meet once or twice a week for four to six weeks and often cost as little as $25.

Another way to manage your time is to determine your peak time of day. This simply involves knowing when you're at your personal best. Perform your most difficult tasks during this period so that when your energy wanes, you can do mindless tasks such as checking the mail, filing documents, or organizing things. You can perform difficult tasks faster and with greater accuracy when you're at your peak, thus saving rework time later.

Prioritize Tasks and Activities

Are you working on important things or just whatever comes along? If the latter is the case, step back and review the priority list you wrote earlier. If others' priorities are always ahead of yours, you'll never lead a balanced, organized life. Spending time with your child discussing how things are going at school, or listening to a spouse or friend who's had a bad day or who just wants to talk are far more important than doing the dinner dishes or folding the laundry. In prioritizing, always put people before things/tasks. Housework, reports, and errands won't disappear if left undone, but a damaged relationship can have long-lasting effects.

Delegate – Overcome the Superwoman Syndrome

Women often feel as if we have to be in charge. We think that if we don't do a task it won't get done or won't be done correctly. Well, take off your bodysuit and cape!!! The world won't come to an end because you didn't do it. Delegate as many tasks as possible—at work and at home. If the job can't be totally delegated, keep only those tasks that you must personally perform. Use the time you free up to do important tasks or other tasks that only you can complete. Here are a few tips on delegating and saving time:

• Cook dinner and have someone else clean the kitchen. If you have teenagers, let them help cook. When you've had a long, tiring day, simply order take-out and go to bed early.

• Assign age-appropriate chores to all family members weekly. Rotate chores to alleviate boredom or perceived unfairness with the undesirable chores. Even if tasks aren't done the way you would have done them, let it go and enjoy the help.

• Avoid clutter by putting files, tools, etc., in their proper places after use to avoid creating piles to be cleaned up later. It also saves time wasted searching for items when they're needed again.

• Don't handle papers over and over. When you receive a document, decide immediately if it needs to be acted upon and when, passed on to someone else, filed or trashed. Avoid making unnecessary piles at your workstation.

• Get on board with technology. Have people send documents electronically. Then set up folders on your computer in which to file them rather than having to keep up with paper copies.

Take Care of Mind, Body and Spirit

One of the most underestimated aspects of life organization is the importance of self-care. Women are notorious for self-neglect. Taking care of oneself makes a significant difference in overall effectiveness. Running on empty and not taking a break has a negative impact on you, your family, and your work. Sometimes women may resort to handling this overload in destructive ways such as overindulgence in alcohol, drugs or food. Self-care must become one of your highest priorities so that you can feel centered and calm and be at your best to nourish your interpersonal relationships. The following are examples of techniques that will assist you in your self-care efforts.

Mind

• Read professional journals, newspapers, magazines, books, etc.
• Take a class or attend a seminar on a topic of interest—personal or professional.
• Engage in thought-provoking activities such as crossword puzzles, trivia, or board games.
• Conduct research on a topic of interest.

Body

• Exercise regularly.
• Eat a balanced diet.
• Get sufficient rest.
• Have fun/laugh often.
• Have regular checkups.
• Take a vacation (good for the mind, body, and spirit).
• Practice deep-breathing to stay alert and relaxed.
• Get outdoors often.

Spirit

• Get involved with an organized faith-based institution.

• Join a social organization.

• Meditate.

• Go on a self-retreat (movie, park, beach, candlelight bath, watch a sunrise/sunset).

• Keep a personal journal.

• Read inspirational literature.

• Serve others. Volunteering will increase feelings of self-worth.

Action Plan for an Organized Life

Review your rankings of the five life activities at the beginning of the chapter.

• Would you still rank them in the same order? _____

• Why or why not? _____

I mentioned earlier that there was no "correct" order, but I encourage you to think carefully about this. Work should never come before any of the other categories on the list. Taking care of your health and spirituality should be top priorities, as they give you the wherewithal to take care of everything else in your life. Work is not your life; it's just a means of making a living. I invite you to review the following as one way to prioritize the five categories: health, spirit, family, friends, and work. Keep this in mind as we move to developing your personal action plan.

Your plan should have the following components: mission statement, objectives, strategies, and maintenance. The flowchart on the following page will help you to create an action plan.

Most of us make work plans all the time, but few see the necessity or take the time to make personal action plans to organize our lives. The old saying, "If you fail to plan, plan to fail," holds true for our personal lives as well. If we fail to set priorities and take control of our own destiny, then we must accept whatever happens to us. Living an organized, balanced life takes intentional and well-thought-out planning. Juggling work, family, and personal issues is a part of life for women. It's not likely to change, but how you handle these issues can. The tips, ideas, and techniques presented in this chapter are tools that can get you started in creating a balanced, organized life without the stress of conflicting demands. For life is much more than a series of unimportant events. Life is what you want it to be and you can have the life you desire if you take control.

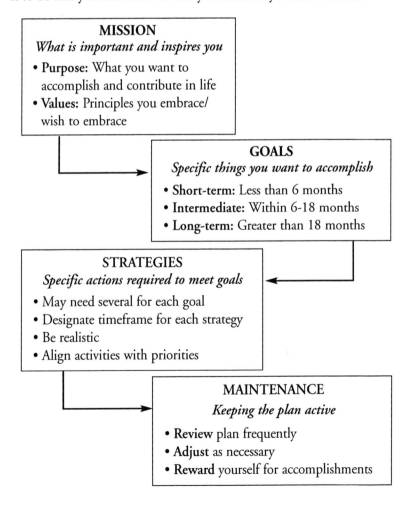

MISSION
What is important and inspires you
- **Purpose:** What you want to accomplish and contribute in life
- **Values:** Principles you embrace/ wish to embrace

GOALS
Specific things you want to accomplish
- **Short-term:** Less than 6 months
- **Intermediate:** Within 6-18 months
- **Long-term:** Greater than 18 months

STRATEGIES
Specific actions required to meet goals
- May need several for each goal
- Designate timeframe for each strategy
- Be realistic
- Align activities with priorities

MAINTENANCE
Keeping the plan active
- **Review** plan frequently
- **Adjust** as necessary
- **Reward** yourself for accomplishments

ABOUT THE AUTHOR

Dr. Danita Johnson Hughes

Danita Johnson Hughes is President and Chief Executive Officer of Edgewater Systems for Balanced Living, Inc., a comprehensive human services provider organization specializing in behavioral health and child welfare services and located in Gary, Indiana. She is the only African American President/CEO of an Indiana Division of Mental Health certified community mental health center in the state of Indiana. Prior to joining Edgewater Systems, she held various positions in the behavioral health and human services fields.

Dr. Hughes is a graduate of Indiana University with both Bachelor's and Master's degrees in Public Administration. She also holds a Master's degree in Social Service Administration and a graduate certificate in Health Administration and Policy from the University of Chicago. Dr. Hughes graduated with a Ph.D. in Human Services from Walden University.

Danita Johnson Hughes is President of The Johnson Hughes Group and has been certified by The Professional Woman Network, an international training organization specializing in helping clients to achieve their leadership potential. Dr. Hughes' areas of expertise include leadership development, women's issues, and issues related to strengthening families and children. Dr. Hughes' training and consulting style as well as her motivational/inspirational speaking talents have received excellent reviews. She is the author of *Power from Within: Discovering What You Already Have to Live Successfully.* She is a regular columnist for the *Post Tribune Newspaper.*

Contact:
Edgewater Systems for Balanced Living, Inc.
P.O. Box 2877
Gary, IN 46403
(219) 881-2460
danitahughes@edgewatersystems.org
www.protrain.net

TWENTY-FIVE

LEADING THE WAY

By Dr. Danita Johnson Hughes

What do we really know about leadership? Leading is not easy. Good leaders are rare and great ones are worth their weight in diamonds. The big question for you is can you, as a leader, take your ideas, your passions, and work with the contrary forces that life throws your way? Your success or failure as a leader relies on your ability to apply your best-laid plans in what the old Chinese saying calls "interesting times." And times are always interesting–never simple, never easy.

Leadership involves convincing people that change is necessary and yet change, even the best kind imaginable, brings with it a certain amount of pain. Thus the question for the leaders is: can I get people to go with me and accept the pain, discomfort, and the "shock of the new" to get to a better place?

It's about them

Without followers, there are no leaders. Many would-be leaders forget this. They become wrapped up in their great ideas and in the ways they will solve difficult problems by the sheer force of their will. That's not what leadership is.

The secret of a leader lies in her ability to get people to follow her on a challenging journey to a new, unknown place that is far outside the usual comfort zone.

You can have the most fantastic, innovative ideas in the world and if you cannot succeed in getting the buy-in of those you are attempting to lead, then all your efforts will ultimately fall short. Former Democratic candidate for President, Howard Dean, had a motto that he quoted many times on the campaign trail. The motto was: "It's the people, stupid!" Dean was reinforcing what every leader should have burned into her mind. It's about the people you are attempting to lead. A leader by definition has people behind her. If she does not, she is not a leader. A leader must spend huge amounts of time considering the landscapes of the minds and hearts of the people she is trying to lead.

Some considerations a leader should make about those they wish to lead:

Who are "they?" Are they senior, junior, or at my level? Are they young or have they been around the block? What do they like to do for fun? Are they stressed out or engaged and happy? What frightens them? What empowers them? What are their dreams and their fears? Spend some time getting to know the people you want to lead before you try to lead them.

How will they feel about a new way of doing things? Are they excited about a novel approach or are they afraid or even belligerent about the idea of change? What push-back are you likely to encounter? Have they "been there, done that?" What concerns and questions will they bring to the table? Have similar ideas or initiatives like yours failed in the past? Always remember that a leader has to know what the people have experienced in their past with your particular organization.

How will they feel about you? What is your track record as a leader? Are you trustworthy? Are you known or unknown to these people? Are you considered a good listener? Are you seen as thoughtful? Will they see you as a know-it-all or will they see you as an innovator? Will they believe that you are keeping their best interests at heart or will they tag you as self-interested? Ask yourself how you would feel if you were being led by you? When it is a question of how others see you, remember that for better or worse, perception is often reality.

You should spend some time seriously considering each of the above. Also, it is imperative that you be brutally honest with yourself. Delusion is a deadly trait in a leader. If you are a bad listener, admit it and start being a good one. If you are unknown to these folks, don't assume they will love you because of your cute outfit. When you truly consider the human side of those you wish to lead, you are well on your way to being a real leader.

Remember that you may have strong opinions on how you want to lead, but the people you want to lead have even stronger feelings about how they want to be led.

Make a Plan…and a Plan B
A good leader will work long and hard to come up with a plan. A great leader knows to also create a Plan B. Effective leaders don't enter the leadership arena saying, "Well, I'll just wing it." A concert pianist or a lead dancer would never even think of hitting the stage without having worked every note of the symphony or every step of the dance to perfection. Not doing so is a sure recipe for disaster. A real leader has considered all the angles, and surprises should be rare for her.

Your plan should be a clear blueprint of your ideas. As discussed above, your plan should include the input of others. Your plan should transform something that is "yours" into something that is "ours."

When you let people have input even over things you may see as trivial, you create group ownership of your idea. Once you find out what people in your group are good at, get their feedback on the plan and then put them to work.

If your community decides to open a new day-care center and you are asked to head up the project, let the person who has a gift for interior design select the furniture for the center. Let the young mother who is a craft artist pick the color schemes and have input on the arts curriculum. Have the carpenter build the shelves. Have the local piano teacher pick out some music that she thinks would be great for the kids. Have the woman who is the CEO of the local bank be the treasurer for the center. If you act like a know-it-all, you will quickly find that you will have to be a do-it-all as well. You will burn out before the task is done.

Your plan should also have one irrefutable characteristic. It should have the boundless ability to change. We have all heard about the folly of the best-laid plans of mice and men. The same goes for the plans of leaders. A great leader is always able to recognize when a plan isn't working the way it should or when a better plan comes along. When you remain open to change, you have the ability to see the entire 360-degree landscape of possibility. When you refuse to consider change, it's like driving down the highway peering through a toilet paper tube.

Be ready for change and welcome it with open arms when it comes.

Surround yourself with supportive people

In America, we have a strange and dysfunctional love affair with the idea of going it alone. We are a country of Marlborough men (and women). Sinatra sang defiantly of doing it "my way." Our notions of leaders are much the same. The central casting version of a leader is an individual who is willing to go it alone, risking all for the glory of being the lone voice of reason and truth. That leader then looks around for her lofty perch only to find that it is lonely at the top. Nothing could be further from the truth.

It turns out that the best leaders very often have an extensive network of people whom they use to help them make decisions. The effective leader knows that wise decisions are not made in a vacuum. Sometimes the person helping the decision-maker is a trusted advisor. Such an individual may have been through the same fires that you find yourself in. Your job as a novice leader is to find those people who can help you and when you discover them, hang onto them for dear life.

There is an important distinction to be made between "yes" people and those who will tell you the cold, hard truth that you need to hear. A supportive person is someone who is a tireless advocate for you and your ideas. But it is important to realize that a supportive person will never let you walk into a leadership situation with a bad idea. Just because someone is an advocate doesn't mean they look at you through rose-colored glasses. A supporter is a realist as well as a cheerleader.

You will find supporters in unlikely places. Some of the best advisors can be found in arenas that have nothing to do with your area of expertise. Some of your most ardent supporters may be found in the ranks of close friends or neighbors. Your minister might be just the person to advise you on questions of leadership in a difficult moral environment. Your neighbor might have some great insight because she really has a way with people.

There are many leaders who will grab anyone to get a differing opinion. They will literally intercept a passer-by to get a new perspective. The more perspectives and opinions you gather, the better your decisions are likely to be. Those ideas will bolster your ideas. In his excellent book, *The Wisdom of Crowds*, author James Surowiecki reveals that decisions made by large groups, with the guidance of a strong leader, are far better than decisions made by an individual or small group. You must ask for—even demand—the help of others. By doing this you will increase your chances of leadership success exponentially.

One thing to be careful of on your hunt for supportive people is the trap of toxic supporters. As you rise to leadership positions, there will be those who will say one thing and do another. These are folks who talk a great game. They will tell you they are all for you and that they are behind you all the way. But they will quietly do everything they can to undercut your effectiveness. I'm sure we've all had people in our families who were examples of toxic support. They may have even thought they loved us but they had a cruel way of cutting us down to size.

Supporters must be selected carefully. If you do find a toxic supporter, don't let them into your inner circle. Be polite. Be civil. But don't be stupid. Keep them at arm's length.

Believe in yourself

It's been said that you're born alone and you die alone. Some people see that as a sad and lonely thing. To me, it is joyous, resounding proof that all of the power and wisdom we need in this life resides within each of us. Each of us has ourselves and that, in some profound way, is more than enough.

I'm not suggesting that we were put on this earth to go it alone. On the contrary, other people are one of the most precious gifts that we are given as leaders and as human beings. People are a tremendous wellspring of love, support, and wise council. That being said, when I think back about the toughest decisions that I've been faced with, in the end, it all came down to me. You will find that it will often be the same for you.

Like it or not, every leader has to make the call when the occasion arises. Experience shows us that letting others make the big choices for us can be ill-advised to say the least. Of course, we've all been there. We've listened to the wrong advice and if we are lucky, we end up with a bad haircut. Unfortunately for those who desire to be leaders, the stakes are often much higher.

Certainly, we may agree on important choices with a life partner or family member or friend. That is what they are there for. But when it all comes down to it, our conscience, our experience, and our expertise must be our ultimate guides. Collectively, they are the sextant that we use to chart our course in a complex world.

In the end, leadership all comes down to you

A great leader trusts others as she trusts herself. She believes in her abilities and in the abilities of those in her peer group. When the critical moment comes, she will be unafraid to act, knowing that she has considered all the angles and personalities. She can take comfort in the council she has sought and in the opinions she has taken into account. In the words of Harvard leadership expert Ron Heifitz, the great leader reaches the critical moment when she must "come down off the balcony."

If she has done the hard work of assessing the needs of those she desires to lead, if she has crafted a Plan and a Plan B, if she has sought out a positive group of supporters, and if she ultimately has an unshakeable, unquenchable belief in herself, then she is well on her way to becoming a great leader. It is a long, steep process with no shortcuts. If leadership was easy, there would only be leaders with no followers. But there is always room for a new generation of leaders.

Great leaders are not born. They are forged from the white-hot fires of life experience.

THE PROFESSIONAL WOMAN NETWORK
Training and Certification on Women's Issues

 Linda Ellis Eastman, President & CEO of The Professional Woman Network, has trained and certified over one thousand individuals to start their own consulting/seminar business. Women from such countries as Brazil, Argentina, the Bahamas, Costa Rica, Bermuda, Nigeria, South Africa, Malaysia, and Mexico have attended trainings.

Topics for certification include:
- Diversity & Multiculturalism
- Women's Issues
- Women: A Journey to Wellness
- Save Our Youth
- Teen Image & Social Etiquette
- Leadership & Empowerment Skills for Youth
- Customer Service & Professionalism
- Marketing a Consulting Practice
- Professional Coaching
- Professional Presentation Skills

If you are interested in learning more about becoming certified or about starting your own consulting/seminar business contact:

The Professional Woman Network
P.O. Box 333
Prospect, KY 40059
(502) 566-9900
lindaeastman@prodigy.net
www.prowoman.net